LOOKING FORWARD

T0071154

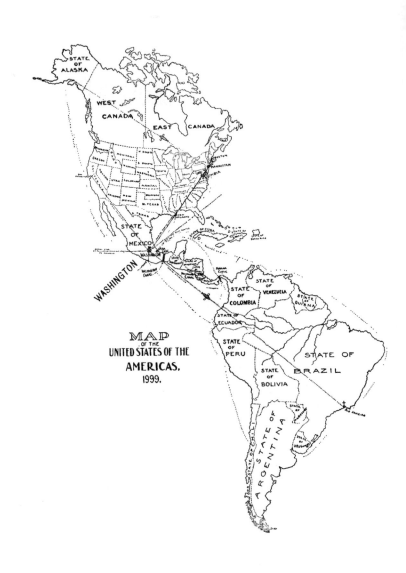

MAP
OF THE
UNITED STATES OF THE
AMERICAS,
1999.

LOOKING FORWARD

—A Dream of the—

United States of the Americas

in 1999

BY ARTHUR BIRD

Skyhorse Publishing

Skyhorse Publishing books may be purchased in bulk at special discounts for sales promotion, corporate gifts, fund-raising, or educational purposes. Special editions can also be created to specifications. For details, contact the Special Sales Department, Skyhorse Publishing, 307 West 36th Street, 11th Floor, New York, NY 10018 or info@skyhorsepublishing.com.

Skyhorse® and Skyhorse Publishing® are registered trademarks of Skyhorse Publishing, Inc.®, a Delaware corporation.

Visit our website at www.skyhorsepublishing.com.

10 9 8 7 6 5 4 3 2 1

Library of Congress Cataloging-in-Publication Data is available on file.
ISBN: 978-1-62636-408-0

Printed in the United States of America

PREFACE.

THE author respectfully submits it as his firm and immovable conviction, that the United States of America, in years to come, will govern the entire Western Hemisphere.

The Stars and Stripes which never knew, nor ever will know defeat, will, in years to come, gather under its protecting folds, every nation and every island in this hemisphere.

It is a duty we Americans owe to the republics of Central and South America to give them the benefits of our pacific government, the rule of the People, by and for the People, exemplified in the great Constitution of the United States of America.

America has to-day an inviolable Monroe Doctrine. Any attempt on the part of Europe to violate the spirit or letter of that wise doctrine, would be promptly resented by America.

Our American flag already protects and defends every republic in the Americas. How many years will it require to convince

the Central and South American Republics
that their security and path of safety is to
come under the flag that already protects
them ?

The purpose of this book is to clearly establish this important fact in the mind of
every patriotic American.   Our glorious,
starry banner will rule the entire Western
Hemisphere.   It will be the emblem of
Peace, Liberty and Civilization, floating
over a united America from Alaska to Patagonia.   This is America's Destiny.

In setting forth this great truth the
author has avoided the well beaten paths
and dusty roads travelled by writers from
the days of the Deluge up to the hour of
going to press, and it is to be hoped that the
reader, now and then, may find some refreshing scenery along his pathway.

If this book serves to stimulate patriotic
pride and strengthen respect for our liberty-
loving flag, it then will not have been written in vain.

Most respectfully submitted,

THE AUTHOR.

LOOKING FORWARD

—— A Dream of——

THE UNITED STATES OF THE AMERICAS,

1999.

CHAPTER I.

THE AMERICAN COLOSSUS.

A Dream of Magnificent Expansion.   America becomes the Mightiest Nation of the World and ex-
tends her Domain from Alaska to Patagonia.

GAUGED by certain standards and viewed from certain standpoints, a mere century is but a brief compass of time.

From an individual point of view, in the daily routine of life, a century appears to be an embryo-eternity.   When time is gauged with clock like precision and to each minute is allotted its full value, a century assumes an unfathomable depth.   But, in the cycles of time, a century is a mere footprint in the passage of time ; a small link in the endless chain of eternity.

Time is easily annihilated by mental process.   Witness the feat performed by Mahomet, related in a certain chapter of the

Mahomet on Rapid Transit.

Koran.   The faithful are informed in this passage of the Koran that the Prophet was awakened one morning from a deep, refreshing slumber by an angel and was summoned into Paradise to confer with Allah.   While in the act of ascending to Heaven, Mahomet's foot struck and upset a pitcher of water which stood near the couch.   The Koran unblushingly proclaims that the Prophet held 999 long conferences with Allah and had safely returned to his couch, ready for another snooze, before the water in the falling pitcher had time to spill on the floor !

There is something very refreshing in this narrative.   It shows that Mahomet was well up in rapid transit matters and again it proves the sublime virtue of a man, a son of the desert, a turbaned Washington, who couldn't tell a lie and who resisted the temptation to make this batch of conferences with Allah an even thousand.   Mahomet missed his calling ; he ought to have been a newspaper reporter.

Assuming the prerogatives of the Koran, the author, at one stroke of his pen, proposes to annihilate time.   Plunged into a profound slumber he had a dream.   Great men and little men ; the renowned and the ignorant ; the philosopher and the Australian bushman ; quakers and cannibals ; the

prince and the peasant, all these and myriads of others, have had their dreams.
Love's dream has been the theme of all ages,
the burden of songs untold. The dream of
conquest, the dream of ambition and dreams
of every human passion and desire have
throbbed within the human brain.

But the author's dream is not swayed by
human emotions ; it is not the handmaid of
America's Giant Republic, 1999. passion. It is a dream
that unseals the book of
the future and reveals to
the world the colossal,
peace-loving, giant republic of the universe
in the year of our Lord, 1999,

The United States of the Americas, the
mightiest nation ever known in contempo-
raneous history.

It is related that at a national anniversary
celebration dinner, held a few years ago, in
the classic regions of Chicago, while the
toasts were being dissected, a guest arose
and proposed to "Our Country,"—the
United States of America, bounded on the
north by Canada ; on the south by the Gulf
of Mexico ; on the east by the Atlantic and
on the west by the Pacific Ocean. Another gentleman arose and protested warmly
against the narrow limits as ascribed
to our beloved country. "Let us," he continued, "drink to the prosperity of the
United States of America,—bounded on the
north by the North Pole ; on the south by
the Antarctic Region ; on the east by the

first chapter of the Book of Genesis and on the west by the Day of Judgment."

At the *fin-de-siecle* of the twentieth century, in the year of our Lord, 1999, the United States of the Americas were virtually bounded as above related.   The comparatively small segment of territory known and officially recognized in 1899 as the United States of America, still retained in 1999 its predominant importance, yet this territory in the twentieth century became only a small fraction of an integral whole.   In 1899, compared with its neighbors, the United States of America appeared like a whale by the side of little fishes,—a large loaf compared with which its neighbor-nations in Central and South America resembled little biscuits,—half baked at that.

In 1999 the little fishes were glad to come to the great American whale for protection and become a part of our grand union. Our glorious and ever-victorious banner remained precisely the same in 1999, as it must ever remain for centuries yet unborn, the pride of America and the glory of the world.   The stripes on our noble flag were still red and white alternately ; the only difference was in the number of the stars on the field of blue ; they had increased from forty-five to eight-five and Old Glory proudly waved in 1999 over one mighty united republic from Baffin's Bay to the straits of Magellan.

Place in your hand an acorn.   Pause as

you gaze upon it, consider the mighty giant which slumbers within its bosom. It is only an acorn, —a mere pigmy. Plant it ; watch it as it develops into a mighty, towering oak, which, in its majesty of strength seems to bid defiance to the very heavens. Beneath its massive branches and grateful shade the weary traveller may pause to rest his limbs and seek refuge from the heat of day.

Our pilgrim fathers were the "acorns" of the colossal republic known in 1999 as **Commenced on a Small Scale.** the United States of the Americas. Little did they those pure and sturdy fathers, dream that from their loins would spring the greatest and grandest government descended to men since the promulgation of the Decalogue. From small beginnings, great ends may often be accomplished. The avalanche that rolls and thunders down the mountain side, sweeping before it forests and boulders, begins business in a very small way. A little handful of snow starts the uproar but before its headlong career has terminated, the very mountain itself trembles beneath the mad rush.

So it was with that splendid political structure, known in 1999 as the United States of the Americas. Its humble origin was easy traceable to Plymouth Rock. From the landing of the pilgrims to the close of the nineteenth century, the rapid growth of the Federal States left nothing to be desired.   But in the nineteenth century America was still an acorn, from which a mighty oak was to be reared in 1999, a tree under whose branches were sheltered in one mighty republic all the territory from Hudson's Bay to Cape Horn.

In the year of our Lord 1999 the world gazed with an admiration, akin to awe, up-

Eighty-five States in the Union. on the magnificient spectacle presented by the United States of the Americas, a colossal republic, embracing eighty-five states, bounded on its northern apex by the states of Alaska, East and West Canada, while the state of Patagonia guarded the extreme south of the American giant, including all islands of the seas lying in the Western Hemisphere, between the Arctic and Antarctic regions.

It frequently happens that the insignificant child of to-day, soon becomes, by reason of growth and intellectual force, the leader of the family, a tower of might and strength in their midst, one to whom they look for counsel and protection.

So it was with America, the Child of Destiny.   In 1776 America was a mere infant, attached to the breast of a harsh, unloving mother.   By leaps and bounds this American infant budded into childhood, and in the year of 1899 had already become a busy, good-natured youth, whose prowess, industry and great future already commanded the respect of the world. In 1899 the western hemisphere was politically divided into independent republics. with the minor exception of certain European dependencies, belonging to England, France and Denmark. The United States in the year last named was universally regarded as a prodigy in the family of nations. Its magnificent resources and its expanding industries; its keen inventive genius; its limit-

A Big Fellow, Decidedly. less agricultural wealth; its absolute liberty and entire freedom from militarism, challenged the envy as well as the admiration of the world, while the naval and military prowess of the young American Republic, evidenced in the Spanish–American unpleasantness of 1898, exacted from other nations a wholesome and enduring respect.

Such, in brief, was the condition of America in 1899. Little indeed was the popular mind prepared for the extraordinary developments and the remarkable series of events that brought about in 1999 the creation of the United States of the Americas. In that memorable year all of the independent republics of Central and South America had joined our union and were governed under the great Constitution of 1776, which is and always will be, the most inspiring document that ever issued from the pen of man, one that will continue to bless mankind as long as the sun re-

tains its power and the earth gives forth its
fruits.

How did all this happen ?   The Dream
furnishes the solution.   Read on.

CHAPTER II.

UNDER THE EAGLE'S WING.

The Mighty Oregon and the Little Yankee Schooner met on the high seas. "Let us keep together for mutual protection." Mexico the first republic to join our union. The Central and South American Republics all stampede for the shelter of the great American Eagle. Peru joins our union in 1921, Venezuela in 1925, Canada comes stumbling along in 1930.

EVERY American patriot recollects with feelings of pride and admiration the great voyage of the U. S. battleship Oregon, the noblest floating citadel of the nineteenth century, during the spring of the year 1898, from the Golden Gate to Jupiter, Florida, a distance of over 14,000 miles. With only five first-class battleships to its credit, it was of paramount importance for the U. S. government to secure the services of the Oregon to join in the volcanic welcome that awaited the arrival of Admiral Cervera's squadron in the Caribbean sea.

The memory of that eventful voyage will remain vivid in the recollections of more than one generation. After the noble vessel had rounded the turbulent waters of Magellan and her stout prow pointed north, anxiety for her safety increased at every knot she covered. The Spanish phantom, at that critical period of the war, looked like a towering mountain, an elevation, however, which was designed to be soon transformed, by subsequent events, into a mole-hill.

One bright afternoon, while steaming in latitude 30° south and in longitude 40° **A Saucy** west, shortly before **Little** touching at Rio Janerio, **Yankee Craft.** the great Oregon spoke an insignificant, one-masted little schooner, a mere shell, tossing upon South Atlantic billows, with a crew of two men. The fact that the diminutive sail boat proudly unfurled at her mast-head the glorious flag of America, was the sole feature, in her case, that saved her from utter insignificance. The Oregon displayed signals, asking the captain of the little vessel if he had spoken any Spanish war-vessels adding, as a matter of information, that war had been declared between Spain and the United States of America.

It happened that this was the first intimation the captain of the schooner had received that a state of war existed between the two countries above named. In reply he promptly signalled to the Oregon that he had not seen any Spanish men-of-war, and, being somewhat of a Yankee humorist, added, that if war had been declared, the best thing that they could do would be "to keep together for mutual protection."

This anecdote of the recontre of the Ore-

"LET US KEEP TOGETHER FOR MUTUAL PROTECTION."

gon and the tiny schooner illustrates aptly the conditions that ruled in 1999 and during several preceding decades. In that year was witnessed a grand union of all the peoples of the Western Hemisphere under the starry banner of America. The little Republics of Central and South America were heartily glad to seek the protection of the Great Leviathan of the North, and, gathered into one great Republic, *The United States of the Americas*, they stood together one and indivisible, '' for mutual protection.''

In 1999 the world beheld the imposing spectacle of a United America, a nation in magnitude and power that eclipsed any previously known confederation of States, invincible in war and unrivalled in arts, sciences and industry. The Americas were all under the protection of the same stars and stripes, employing the same legal tender and coinage and in 1999 the English tongue had been adopted officially by every Central and South American State.

The first Republic that knocked at our gates for admission into the grand union of the Americas, was Mexico. In the year 1520, the Spaniards, under Cortes, that valiant and most intrepid of Castillian warriors, had already crushed that most dreaded of all barbarian monarchs, Montezuma, and had reduced the Aztec Empire into vassalage

Mexico makes the First Break.

and slavery. In 1898, by a series of the most brilliant victories, American prowess and arms, coupled with dare-devil bravery and resolute fighting, had in turn driven out the Spanish hordes from the Americas. With this turn in the tide of history, nothing could be more fitting than the incorporation of Mexico as a State in our Federal Union. Could they have witnessed our brilliant American victories against Spain in 1898, Montezuma and his Aztec warriors would have arisen from their graves and shouted for joy at the knowledge that at last their wrongs at the hands of Spain had been avenged by the sword of America and their Spanish oppressors of 1520 had at last been hurled back to the Castillian haunts from whence they had emerged under Columbus and Cortes.

Mexico added a new star to our flag in 1912, just one hundred years after England and America crossed swords. These swords have been sheathed in their scabbards, never again in the word's history to be unsheathed against one another.

As early as the year 1899 the desire to join our American Union began to manifest itself. In that year the **Awakening of the Americas.** little island of Jamaica already had under advisement the question of joining the American Union, and the people of Jamaica were seriously agitating the matter. They regarded this step as one that would benefit their material prosperity. This belief was shared by the inhabitants of the other West Indian islands and gained strength with every year, culminating in 1912 in the action taken by Mexico.

The incorporation of Mexico into our grand American Union created a profound sensation, not only in the Americas, but, also, throughout the world. It was a purely voluntary act on the part of Mexico, one which could not be fondly ascribed by the ever-jealous nations of Europe to " Yankee greed." It brought about a distinctive turn in the tide and the conviction became firm in the minds of all that the example of Mexico would be followed, sooner or later, by every Republic in Central and South America.

In 1920 public opinion in Peru became ripe for a change. The affairs of that Republic had been unsuccessfully administered and the land of the Incas seemed likely in that year to be devastated by Chile, that active and more or less prosperous people, sometimes called the "Yankees of South America." The prospect of another disastrous war with Chile crystalized public opinion in Peru and hastened action on her part. In the following year of 1921, Peru became a State in our Union. Venezuela came next in 1925, then followed in rapid succession the entire group of Central American States, Guatemala, Salvador, Nicaragua, Costa Rica, Honduras.

In 1930 Canada at last joined the American Union. Canada had long occupied the position of an old maid in reference to the Union ; she had been entirely willing for many years, but had withheld her consent ; England, of course, had to be consulted, and with the utmost good nature was present at the wedding ceremonies, giving away the Canadian bride into our union in a most gracious manner.

Between 1930 and 1935, in rapid succession, the entire stretch of territory known as South America, and the eleven Republics occupying that continent, were incorporated into the United States of the Americas. The State of Brazil was recognized by Congress in 1931, and, on account of its large area, consisting of 3,209,878 square miles, the new State was styled the "Texas of the South."

During the last half of the nineteenth century the burning issues caused by the

Old Wounds are Healed Up. Civil War were generally and vaguely characterized as those which existed between the North and South. The question of State sovereignty, slavery and the resultant Civil War, divided the North and South into two vast, hostile camps. The fall of Richmond in 1865 terminated hostilities, it is true, but a bitter, relentless political and social war was waged between these sections for over a quarter of a century thereafter. The deep wounds caused by the Civil War began to slowly heal, but it required a foreign war to demonstrate to the world that time at last had conquered all animosity, all the anguish and bitterness of spirit that had existed between the North and South.

During our war with Spain from April 22, 1898, to October 26, of the same year, Confederate generals who had taken prominent parts in the Southern army, men who had led their hosts to help tear into tatters the great Constitution of the United States, unsheathed their swords once more, in 1898, and to their lasting honor, this time it was in defense of that very Constitution.   In 1898 the men of the South eagerly followed the lead of Wheeler and Fitzhugh Lee and sprang to arms in the defence of a united country.   It was a most impressive spectacle ; one that filled the world with amazement and America with patriotic joy.

In 1999, that little strip of territory lying between Mason and Dixon's line and the **No more "South" in 1999.** gulf of Mexico was no longer known or recognized as the South. The sceptre of the South had passed into the keeping of the South American continent, which territory in 1999 had been divided into ten States of our great American Union, namely the States of Venezuela, Brazil, Ecuador, Colombia, Chile, Paragua, Uruagua, Bolivia, Peru and, in the extreme South, the State of Patagonia.

The real and actual South of the United States of the Americas, in 1999, consisted of the States above named, a vast sweep of territory lying between the 10 ° North and 55 ° South of the equator, embracing 8,207,688 square miles in area, with a population of 127,000,000 souls. In 1999 the State of Brazil alone had a population of 42,000,000.

The Middle States of the great American Republic in 1999 were those of Central America, namely the States of Costa Rica, Salvador, Honduras, Guatemala, Nicaragua and Mexico.

The Northern States of the great Republic in 1999 consisted of those states lying between Alaska and the Mexican gulf, including the newly acquired States of East and West Canada. The population of the Middle States in 1999 was estimated at 75,000,000, while the census of the Northern States figured at 329,000,000. The total population of the United States of the Americas in 1999, figured at 531,000,000 souls.

CHAPTER III.

THE CUBAN QUESTION SETTLED.

The wretches who blew up the Maine. America is
slow to anger but terrible in punishment. Cuban
native government not a success. Joins our
Union in 1910.

CUBA became part of the United States
in 1910. The direct cause of the war
of 1898 was the blowing up of the Maine.
Through this premeditated and diabolical
act, no less than 266 of our brave American
sailors were murdered in cold blood.

The Madrid authorities were innocent
parties to this lamentable transaction and
their representative in Havana, Captain-
General Blanco, has been acquitted of the
heinous charge of participation in that
fearful piece of butchery. The guilty men,
the assassins who blew up the Maine on the
night of the 15th of February, 1898, were
Weylerites, whose chief, the infamous Gen.
Weyler, had been removed from office by
the Sagasta government. To resent this
slight upon their chief ; to embroil their
home government in a war with the United
States, and to gratify their thirst for American blood, these Weylerites, (who themselves located the mines in Havana harbor,)
watched their opportunity and exploded the
mine that destroyed our gallant vessel, hurling into eternity 266 of as brave men as ever
trod a deck.

But the vengeance that was meted out to Spain for the treachery of her murderous **The Maine was Avenged.** sons, was sweeping and most complete in its character. Our martyrs of the Maine have been avenged. Spain has learned along with the rest of the nations, that America is slow to anger but swift and terrible in her vengeance; from the punishment of Spain the world has learned a Yankee lesson that will be remembered in all time to come.

Apart, however, from the castigation of Spain, America had a duty to perform in the liberation of Cuba. From the date of the arrival of the first shipload of Spaniards in 1492 to the departure of the last load of Spanish officials and soldiers in 1899, Cuba had rested under a cloud. Prosperity under Spanish rule, from Valesque in 1510 to Blanco in 1898, appeared to be an impossibility. From Christopher Columbus to Admiral Cervera, the first and the last Spanish navigators despatched by the crown of Spain to Cuba, the life-blood of that fair isle had been wasted away. Its history may fitly be written in blood. Such condition of affairs could not be endured always at the threshold of a vast, liberty-loving Republic and Cuba's loud appeals for aid stirred America to action. War was declared after a formal demand upon Spain for the liberation of Cuba. The result of the war of 1898 was that Spain stood up to the front just long enough to get kicked into tatters.

On the 1st day of January, 1902, the military occupation of Cuba by the troops **A Civil War in Cuba.** of the United States terminated and the government passed into the keeping of the Cubans. The Cuban government, under President Gomez, was beset with difficulties from the start. It was found difficult to bridle and keep down jealousies and partisan feelings among the Cubans themselves. They appeared to detest one another under their native government as cordially as they did their former task-masters, the Spaniards. As soon as the Cubans established their own government, love of country vanished from among them ; there appeared to be no unity of purpose.

In 1907 a civil war broke out in the fair but unfortunate isle, and during the summer of that year the terrible scenes of the last struggle with Spain, under Weyler, were again re-enacted. During that year and the two following years of 1908–09, the gleaming machette once again performed its deadly work.

This fratricidal war came to an end early in 1910, when the Cubans by a plebicite, or popular vote, rendered an almost unanimous vote in favor of the annexation of Cuba to the United States. This important decision was ratified by Congress and received the official signature of President George Dewey, the hero of Manila, at noon on the 24th day of December, 1910.

CHAPTER IV.

KEYNOTE OF AMERICAN EXPANSION.

The Awakening of America. Dewey the Idol of a
great Nation. His immense responsibilities at a
critical period of the war. In 1999 Manila is still
on every tongue. Spain's bargain with Germany. Discomfiture of the German Admiral

IT was the first gun of the Raleigh, fired
in Manila bay at dawn on the first day
of May, 1898, that sounded the keynote of
America's future greatness. The echo of
that gun had not died out even in 1999.
It still rang amidst the nations of the earth,
reverberating across its seas and continents. It was the signal that sounded the
dawn of

The United States of the Americas,
a mighty Republic, which, in the year 1999,
embraced every square foot of land in the
Western Hemisphere, from the snow-clad
huts of the Esquimos to the rock-ribbed
straits of Magellan, with its teeming, hustling population of 531,000,000 souls.
Uncle Samuel was boss of the ranch, from
its Patagonian cellar clear to its roof in the
Arctic region. With its mighty talons
clutching the narrow isth-
mus of Panama ; with its
beak pointing into the
Atlantic, far beyond

**The Great
Bird
of Freedom.**

Porto Rico ; with its tail-feathers covering
the expanse of the Pacific, clear into the

Philippines, the American Eagle was a proud bird to behold, as its mighty wings spread from the North to the South Pole. And Dewey's guns did it.

At critical periods the fate of nations, as well as of individuals, seems to suspend by a single, slender thread. At such moments, so keenly poised are the balances of fate, that a mere breath may disturb them. Admiral Dewey, the idol of America, unknowingly, held the fate of a vast Republic in the hollow of his hand. He knew it not ; America knew it not. But in the light of events in 1999 such proved to be the case. Had he failed ; had his brave squadron been annihilated by treacherous mines in Manila bay ; had our American fleet been destroyed at Cavité, instead of Montojo's squadron, the Dream of the United States of the Americas would not have been realized in 1999.

But America is unconquerable ; and Dewey won. When, on the 24th day of April, 1898, the momentous message flashed across sea and continent to Dewey, ordering him to "sink or capture" the Spanish squadron, the American Eagle gave its first shrill cry of defiance. Every man on the American fleet off Hong Kong swelled with pride from Commodore Dewey to the humblest powder-monkey. Theirs was a mission to feel proud of, and when Dewey's six warships sailed south to Manila, April 27, 1898, to interview the Castillians, every man on board the American squadron was ready to lay down his life in the cause of our noble country.

These were the men with cool heads and unflinching bravery who first encountered the Spanish hosts   These were the men who electrified a whole world by the splendor of their matchless victory.   The word gratitude is a feeble one indeed to adequately express the feelings of the American people when the truth became known.   At first it seemed incredible that such a brilliant stroke could have been accomplished in less than ten days after the declaration of war. In 1999 men occasionally referred to Trafalgar and the battle of the Nile, Farragut's heroism at Mobile bay, the encounter of those two little scorpions, the Monitor and Merrimac, and other naval engagements, as matters of history, but the peerless American victory at Manila bay, the praises of the one and only Dewey and his brave men, were still, in that year, the theme on every tongue.

In 1999 it was reckoned a high distinction for any American to be able to say that his father, brother or relative took part in the great victory at Manila.   Indeed, there still lived in 1999, in the State of Brazil, an extremely old man, aged 115 years, who took part in the gallant fight off Cavité in 1898.

When Dewey's squadron left Mirs bay to proceed upon its eventful voyage to Manila,

Earl Stanley, at that time a stripling of fourteen years, hid in an empty hogs-

A Plucky Little American Lad. head in the hold of the warship Boston, just as the American fleet was weighing anchor. When the mountains about Mirs bay and the Chinese mainland had disappeared from the sight of the squadron, Stanley, the young stowaway, emerged from his retreat and soon after landed in the arms of a marine, who brought the lad before the Captain. That official was at first inclined to deal severely with the young culprit. The latter, however, was straightforward and fearless in his bearing. He plainly told the Captain that he stole his way on board the Boston to share in the fight and he was ready to do anything to fight under the Stars and Stripes. The Captain, though outwardly severe, secretly admired the lad's pluck and turned him over to the charge of a gun-crew. In 1999 Earl Stanley resided in Rio Janeiro, and for over sixty years had been drawing a month-ly pension of $35 from the government. He was in that year the sole survivor of the battle of Manila, an exclusive distinction he had already enjoyed for many long years.

Aside from the sweeping results of the action off Cavité, Admiral Dewey's firm and resolute attitude towards Aguinaldo and his mercenaries, as well as his open defiance to

the German squadron, gave the keenest sat-
isfaction throughout the United States.

As early as the year 1902, the fact, long
suspected, was at last officially confirmed,
that before the declaration of war in 1898

**Spain failed
to deliver
the Goods.**
between Spain and Amer-
ica, there existed a firmly
established secret alliance
between Spain and Ger-
many. Spain had bartered with Germany
for her active support in her war against
the Yankees. In compensation for her aid
and countenance, Spain had agreed to cede
over to Germany, in fee simple, the entire
group of Philippine islands. After Dewey's
matchless victory of the 1st of May, Germany slipped on her "thinking cap" and
experienced an exceedingly sudden change
of mind. Her "aid" in the Spanish cause
was not worth a baby's rattle. As to the
German "countenance," it looked so crest-
fallen and hopelessly sour that Spain as she
gazed upon it refused to be comforted.

But, notwithstanding this, with an impu-
dence that was positively refreshing to
contemplate, after the battle of Manila,
Germany put up a fine game of bluff and
acted as though she held a proprietary interest in the Philippines. The German
government dispatched a fleet of seven war
vessels to Manila bay, under command of
Admiral von Diederichs, under a flimsy pretext of "protecting German interests." In
reality it was intended by the presence of

this German squadron in Manila bay to annoy, bulldoze, and if possible to intimidate Commodore Dewey.

For six weeks after the battle of Manila, Dewey's fleet as a result of the fight, was **Little Powder but lots of Pluck.** low in its ammunition and coal supplies. There was one very important fighting factor however, that never ran short on the American fleet, as that was the indomitable pluck and fighting mettle of Dewey and his men. Dewey diplomatically tolerated some of the petty annoyances offered at that time by the Germans, but they were given by the brave American commander to distinctly understand that there existed a danger-line which once crossed, would bring death and hospitals in its wake. None knew better than the German Admiral that the practice of lighting matches around powder magazines is a very unhealthy one.

Admiral Von Diederichs bluffed around with his squadron, but with a wisdom that Solomon himself might have envied, he gave Dewey's danger-line a wide berth. It was only when Admiral Dewey sent his famous request to the Department for the Oregon, "for political reasons," that the German fleet in Manila bay suddenly discovered that they had some urgent business elsewhere, and made a very hasty exit from the unhealthy neighborhood of an American Admiral who had a mind of his own and a fine lot of lads to back up his opinion.

CHAPTER V.

CENTENNIAL CELEBRATION OF MAN-ILA 1998.

America never surrenders, and that is one reason
why we hold on to the Philippines. Grand
Celebration of the Dewey Centennial throughout the Americas.

IN the year 1999 the American possession
of the Philippine islands was regarded
throughout the United States of the Americas as a master stroke. Statesmen in that
year asked themselves how the Americas
could have ever developed their enormous
Asiatic commerce, without having a *point
d' appui*, or base of operations, in Oriental
waters?

In the year 1899 Christendom (and
Heathendom, as well,) beheld with amazement the carving up of China by the greedy
vultures of Europe. In that year of her
interminable history, China resembled a
huge, helpless jelly-fish, attacked on every
side by the sword-fishes of Europe. While
this interesting process of China-carving
was in full operation, America, as a result
of Dewey's victory, discovered that a pearl

The Philip-pines in 1999.

of rare value had fallen
into her lap. When
Dewey entered Manila
bay on the ever memor-
able morn of May 1st, 1898, he had not so

much as a hitching-post to fasten the paint-
er (rope) of his smallest launch.   But, before the setting of the sun on that day, he
had laid low a whole empire under the keels
of his squadron.   There lived not a solitary
European Admiral of the period of 1898
who would not have given his right arm to
have been in Dewey's place.

In 1999 it appeared incredible that one
year only after the battle of Manila there
were men (earnest and well-meaning patriots, many of them,) who were strenuously
opposed to the retention of those islands
by the United States of America.   It was
difficult, in the twentieth century, to con-
ceive how short-sighted, how unmindful of
our country's glorious future, were those so-
called anti-expansionists.

In 1999 the argument was clear and indisputable that America in 1898 had not
waged a wanton war for conquest.   It was
a necessity of war that brought about the
destruction of the Manila wing of the Spanish fleet, and the city was captured subse-
quently as an act of self-defense.   It became a measure of ne-
Rocked in cessity to " put to sleep "
the Cradle every Spanish gun afloat
of the Deep. in the Pacific.   Had
Dewey allowed any of these sea-hounds to
escape and prey upon American commerce
in that ocean, what would have become of
our merchant shipping in the Pacific ?
Our finest steamships would have been at

the mercy of the most contemptible Spanish privateer.   Hundreds of precious lives
and American shipping, representing millions of dollars, must have been destroyed
by the pirates of the red and yellow flag.
But Dewey put them all to sleep and rocked
them in the cradle of the deep.

This deed of self-defence accomplished,
then what ?   Ought Dewey to have vacated
Manila bay and made a laughing-stock of
himself or stand his ground and bring the
fight with Spain to a finish ?   There can be
but one patriotic answer to this question.

Dewey stood his ground, and in 1899
public opinion throughout the world divided
itself into two great camps—those who
openly and others who secretly admired the
brave American Admiral.

On the 1st day of May, 1998 the Centennial anniversary of the battle of Manila was
celebrated with a volcanic display of intense
enthusiasm throughout the United States of
the Americas.   It was " Dewey Day" from
the State of Alaska clear south to the State
of Patagonia.   The seals
in Baffin's bay wore an
extra smile, while the
albatross and other gulls
at the Horn circled about and fluttered as
though something uncommon was on.

Equal to the 4th of July.

Every city in the vast Republic was in
gala attire to honor the glorious memories
of the day.   In Washington, (Mexico,) and
at the capitals of each of the eighty-five

States of the Americas the Manila Centennial was signalized with a patriotic enthusiasm seldom equaled but never eclipsed.

The celebration of the Centennial anniversary of Waterloo by the old allied nations of Europe in 1915 proved a very brilliant affair, one which dazzled the world by its magnificence and regal splendor. But the Manila Centennial in 1998 relegated the Waterloo episode entirely in the shade. The only American national celebration of the twentieth century that might compare with it was the Bi-Centennial celebration of the Declaration of Independence on the 4th day of July, 1976.

The Manila Centennial in 1998 celebrated what was universally regarded as the pivotal

Turning Point of American History or turning point in American History. From the date of that battle in 1898 the supremacy of the United States became established as a first-grade power. Its prowess in war and triumphs in the arts of peace were universally recognized. Little then is it to be wondered at that the American Colossus in 1998 seethed with patriotic fervor on the 1st day of May of the Manila Centennial anniversary.

The preparations for the great event had been under way for nearly a year. It was clearly remembered in 1998 that, although Bunker Hill was an insignificant fight from a military point of view, yet it was a glori-

ous battle for America from the fact that it
proved a turning point in our nation's history.   So it proved with the battle of Manila.   It was a turning point in our national
history that demanded a fitting celebration
of its centennial anniversary.

In 1998 the President of the United
States of the Americas was Vernon R.

**A Chip
of the
Old Block.**
Schley, a grandson of
the famous Admiral who
annihilated Cervera's
fleet on the 3d day of
July, 1898, while the commander-in-chief
was inconveniently away on some other
errand.   Upon President Schley devolved
the high honor, but irksome and difficult
task, of firing at sunrise a salute of aerial
torpedoes in the capitals of every State in
the vast American Republic, and, at the
same moment, from his private office in the
Capitol building in Washington, Mexico,
the President unfurled the American flag on
the dome of every State house in the
Americas.

This, of course, was accomplished by
means of electricity.   At first thought it
might appear to be a very easy task to press
a button in the State of Mexico and fire off
aerial torpedoes in the States of Alaska, the
Canadas, Peru, Patagonia, Argentine,
Venezuela, Bolivia and Brazil at the same
instant, extending the salutes to the Middle
American States of Nicaragua, Costa Rica,
Salvador, Guatemala, but as a matter of

fact, the task of the President was by no means an easy one.

On the Manila Centennial anniversary day President Schley required nearly three **Going Around with the Sun.** hours of constant work to fire the national salutes from the Eastern to the Western Capitals of the great Republic at exactly sunrise in each city on the 1st day of May, 1998. The sun arose on the Eastern Capitals of the New England States that morning at 5:32 A. M. in Hartford, Boston, Montpelier and other cities, but it was nearly 8:43 A. M. before the President could fire off the aerial torpedoes over the Golden Gate, unfurling at the same moment Old Glory, which waved to the morning breezes of the broad Pacific.

All those States of the Americas, from Canada to Patagonia that are on the same degree of longitude received their signals from the President at about the same time. The most easterly city of the American Union in 1999 was Rio Janeiro, situate on the 40 ° longitude. The torpedo salutes were first fired there in honor of the great Centennial. The next city that saluted was Montevideo. Buenos Ayres next followed. Boston, Mass., Caracas in the State of Venezuela and Bogota in the State of Colombia were next ''touched off'' by President Schley, and so in the course of the rising sun each American city saluted the glorious day. When this feature of the 1998 centennial program was explained to a Frenchman on the 1st day of May of that year, he shrugged his shoulders as only a Frenchman can, exclaiming : "Mon Dieu, vhy don't zey fire a salute in zee sun,—parbleu."

In this vast aggregation of eighty-five States the Dewey Centennial celebration was everywhere observed with marked enthusiasm, but the style of the celebration differed widely, according to the section or location of the State in which it was held.

Different Ways of Celebrating. Throughout Alaska and the two Canadian States and the northern belt of States, military pageants, naval parades, athletic sports, orations, concerts and banquets predominated.

In the tropical or Central American States, high mass was celebrated in all the cathedrals and churches in Mexico, Honduras, Nicaragua, Salvador, Guatemala and Costa Rica, and the day was given to feasting and dancing. Throughout the southern sections of the United States of the Americas, in Colombia, Venezuela, Brazil and contiguous States, the Te Deum was chanted in all the principal churches and high mass was celebrated with a pomp and magnificence that appeals so irresistibly to the heart of the Latin race. In each State of the Americas ample appropriations had been voted from State funds to meet the expenses of the great day. Not a family in the colossal American Republic of 500,-000,000 souls lacked on that day for a feast of the choicest delicacies, with a carte blanche of wines of the most grateful and generous vintage.

On the occasion of the Manila Centennial in 1999 Englishmen were accorded the seat of honor at every table in the Americas and the health of King Alexander II, who in 1999 wielded the sceptre of Great Britain, was tossed off with gusto and enthusiasm by every living American. England's true and sterling friendship to America in 1898 was still vividly remembered in 1998. The strong grasp of her hand at a critical period in 1898, when her attitude became a matter of vital importance to America, was still cordially appreciated.

Every American Governor in the South American States as well as those of Central and North America, gave a sumptuous banquet in honor of the day. At Rio Janeiro Gov. Day entertained no less than 9,000 at his festive tables. Gov. Horace K. Depew, a grandson of the Senator and ex-railroad magnate, entertained 30,000 guests in Washington, (Mexico). In splendor, elegance and lavish hospitality even the chronicles of the Middle Ages could furnish no parallel. Gov. Depew's guests were banqueted and fêted in one of Montezuma's old palaces which still retained much of its architectural beauty and was rich in the memories of a glorious past.

High mass was celebrated in the cathedral of Mexico. Gov. Depew and a brilliant staff attended the services. All public edifices and private houses were profusely decorated with garlands and festoons of beautiful tropical flowers of the most gorgeous dyes. Massive arches, embellished with medallions of Dewey, were erected on all the principal streets and avenues. These were made of verdant boughs, intertwined with the choicest floral creations of the tropics. Martial music and a constant firing of aerial torpedoes kept public interest at its keenest edge, from dawn to night. These festive scenes in the State of Mexico were re-enacted all over the Americas on the 1st day of May, 1998. The Dewey or Manila Centennial was a tribute to the memory of the man who at Manila bay, electrified the world and laid the corner stone of the United States of the Americas.

Celebrating in Mexico.

CHAPTER VI.

ENGLAND'S VALUED FRIENDSHIP.

The American Victory at Manila was also an English Victory, so proud did our British cousins feel over it. Spain's bribe of the Philippines. France and Germany beg England to remain Neutral while they set out to thrash Uncle Sam.

IF the reader is an American, the question will naturally arise, what became of our transatlantic cousins in the " right tight little island " in the year 1999 ? In what light was the stupendous fabric of the United States of the Americas regarded by England in that year? Did England view with friendliness and complacency the development of the American Colossus ? Surely the awakening of the Americas, both politically and industrially, must have seriously challenged the attention of England. Was England in 1999 the same powerful, cordial friend of America that she so well proved herself to be in 1898 ?

During the year 1899 Admiral Seymour of the British Navy, while cruising in Asiatic waters, paid Admiral Dewey a visit on the Olympia. His parting words to the American Admiral were : " Your victory at Cavité was also our victory." No words could better express the fraternal and cordial relations existing in 1899 between England and America and the Dreamer feels

proud and happy to say that in 1999 these
cordial relations were still in full force.
Providence, it would appear, had selected
these two great nations to act as leaders
and standard-bearers among the peoples of
the earth.   Their spheres of action in 1999
did not clash, hence no jealousy existed between the two nations.

In 1899 America, while perfectly friendly
to England and proud to be her ally, was
reluctant to enter into an offensive and de-
fensive alliance with her.   The spirit of
American independence, always self-reliant,
was slow and exceedingly cautious in the
matter of "entangling alliances."   The
only alliance possible would be one with
England, which nation is the parent of the
Anglo-Saxon race.

England's wise and friendly course during
the Spanish-American war, had filled the
**England
our
Firm Friend.** heart of every true American patriot with grati-
tude.   By her sagacious
action the unpleasant
memories of 1776, 1812 and the Alabama
episode, had been entirely obliterated, root
and branch, from every American breast.

Before the outbreak of hostilities in 1898,
which culminated in the Yanko-Spanko war,
there existed between France, Germany and
Spain a secret, yet none the less tacit un-
derstanding, that in the event of war, the
two powers first named would come forward
to the assistance of Spain as against the

cordially detested Yankees. France held the bulk of Spanish securities and was vitally interested in the issue of the conflict between Spain and America. The success of the Spanish cause or its disaster, signified either the gain or loss of millions of Spanish securities. Her sympathies, therefore, were given over to Spain and the French government and people were quite ready to expend chilled steel and smokeless powder against the bulwarks of America.

Germany, on the other hand, in her self-assumed rôle of general meddler-in-chief of

Spain's Two Great and Good Friends. the so-styled "European concert," was spoiling for a fight with a country that had taken from her hundreds of thousands of her best citizens and whose industrial expansion was a thorn in her side.

For the first time since 1870, when the French tri-color was humbled in the dust of Sedan, Germany and France were interested in a common cause against America, and were actuated by the same selfish motives against the American Republic. Both were ready in April, 1898, to fly at America's throat and in unison with Spain, administer to our American Republic a first-class thrashing. These two worthies entertained the notion that the great American Republic would very soon be humbled and be only too glad to sue for peace on bended knees.

In return for her valuable services in this

delightful program, Germany was to be re-
warded by Spain with the gift outright of
the Philippine islands. This was the beautiful cluster of grapes which tempted the
cupidity of the German fox.

But, alas, in the language of the lament-
ed Josh Billings, "nothing is more certain
than the uncertainty of this world." France
and Germany, (an ill-assorted and graceless
pair,) had reckoned without their host.

Sorely against their wishes, with hat in
hand, France and Germany found themselves under the absolute necessity of calling
at the office of a certain pugnacious and
only too well known gentleman by the name
of John Bull, whose home since the days
of the Druids and William the Bastard has
been in the snug little island of England
and whose postoffice address is London.

They (F. and G.) came to consult John
Bull on the very important subject of their
proposed expedition against America, with
Spain acting as a tail to their kite.

They explained to Mr. Bull the object of
their mission ; they set forth in a very clear
light that Uncle Sam, on
A Very the other side of the At-
Anxious lantic, needed a sound
Pair. thrashing, and what was
more, needed it very badly. France and
Germany posed before J. B. as champions
of a weaker nation that they were both very
anxious to protect. They represented that
they had no possible interest in the outcome

of a war between America and Spain.   All
they asked of England was merely to remain
neutral,—to keep quiet while the three prize
stars, France, Germany and Spain, proceeded to give Uncle Sam a taste of their raw-
hides.

Then it was that the British Lion gave a
roar, and in clear, unmistakable language
informed both France and Germany if they
ventured to fire a gun against America in
the defence of Spain, England would not
remain neutral, but would side with America and lend her assistance on sea and land.

The British Lion is not to be trifled with.
France and Germany knew this only too
well, and when the war broke out they decided to remain home and wisely stay in
doors while it rained   Spain went to war
alone with her powerful enemy and took her
medicine, we were nearly tempted to say,
" like a good little man."

The era of fraternal love, inaugurated
through England's wise action in repulsing
the advances of France and Germany,
proved the keystone to the greatness of
America and England in 1999.   Ever after
the Spanish-American war they remained
loyal and true to one another and their
friendship and mutual interests ever increased thereafter.   Throughout the twentieth century England and America stood
side by side in every emergency.   It was
not necessary to draw up legal documents
with enormous seals and yards of red silk

ribbon to cement the alliance of true friendship that existed between the two nations.
Their hearts beat in unison in the common
cause of humanity.　In the twentieth century England and America were invincible
in war and leaders in all arts of peace.

CHAPTER VII.

OUR FOREIGN RELATIONS IN 1999.

HAVING clearly set forth in our earlier chapters the splendid proportions and the commanding position on this globe held by the United States of the Americas in 1999, it now becomes necessary in order to determine the position of the great American Republic in its international relations, to review, in brief, the condition of Europe, and, more particularly that of England, in the twentieth century.

In the year 1999 the British and American flags protected over one-half of the human family and before the close of the twenty-first century it appeared certain that English would become the universal language. The population of the world in 1999 figured at a trifle over 2,000,000,000 souls. The population of the United States of the Americas in 1999 was rated at 531,000,000, while that of the British possessions figured at about an equal amount, making a grand total population of over 1,000,000,000 people under the flags of the two nations. It is easy to comprehend how, under two thoroughly enlightened governments, **English the Universal Language.** with a good system of education, free schools, and an enterprising press, English rapidly came to the front as the universal language, and in the year 1999 it became obvious and clear to all candid minds that the Anglo-Saxon race already dominated the world.

The Arbitration Treaty between England and America was signed on the 6th day of June 1910. By the provisions of this document it was agreed that in the event of any dispute between the two countries Arbitration as a settlement for all difficulties would be resorted to. Public opinion on both sides of the Atlantic was sternly opposed to any resort to war between England and the Americas. The Arbitration Treaty was signed by her gracious Majesty, Queen Victoria, who was still seated on the British throne and was enjoying a fair measure of health in 1910 at the venerable age of 92 years. This marvelous and well-preserved lady still retained the homage and respect of the entire world, and the indications pointed to a grand celebration of her Majesty's centennial anniversary in 1918. But the world was denied that privilege and honor. In the year 1912, the Duke of York, (Victoria's grandson,) succeeded to the British throne, assuming the title of Alexander I.

In 1999 radical changes had taken place in the map of Europe. The long interna-

France Gobbled Up by Germany. tional feud and bitterness existing between France and Germany had been twice weighed in the scales of war. The wound caused to French

national pride by the fall of Sedan, Metz and Paris, rancored long in the breasts of all Frenchmen. It was a grief silently borne, but none the less keen. In 1907 the French military party again shouted the battle cry, "A Berlin," and in the brief but disastrous war that followed again were the proud eagles of France trailed in the dust. France lost more of her territory in the Franco-German war of 1907 and Germany saddled on her an enormous war indemnity in the shape of $3,000,000,000.

This was a hard blow to French national pride. Russia, her ally, proved false to her promises of aid and France was left alone to determine the issue with Germany.

The terrible disaster of 1907 only added oil to the French fire of hatred, and in 1935 France, for some imaginary cause, again entered into another war of revenge, (guerre de revanche,) against Germany. As a result of the war of 1935 France utterly collapsed. At the close of that war Germany took possession of Paris and maintained German garrisons in all of the forts surrounding that city for a period of **Germans Hold Paris for Ten Years.** ten years, or until the year 1945. Germany determined, while holding possession of Paris, to reduce the enormous military establishment of France, the maintenance of which had greatly impoverished both countries. In order to suppress and crush France, German garrisons were maintained in every province of France. In this manner Germany kept her mailed grasp upon France, ready at any moment to stifle her upon the least show of resistance. In 1999 France became practically reduced to the condition of a German province.

Those who lived in the year 1899 will recollect only too well the crying injustice

The Wrongs of Poor Dreyfus. perpetrated upon the person of an innocent French officer, Dreyfus, who suffered and was humiliated in a manner which, fortunately, seldom falls to the lot of man. France's lack of moral courage to grant justice to Capt. Dreyfus for so many years, proved to the world that " la belle France," after all, was merely a Dead Sea apple,—beautiful to the eye but rotten to the core.

It is then no cause for surprise that France, the moral coward, in 1935, had been transformed into a German province.

In 1999 Spain and Turkey had both been carved up, banqueted upon and digested by

Adieu Spain and Turkey. the political cannibals of Europe. In the partition that took place in the twentieth century England had been careful to secure for herself some of Spain's choice side-cuts and joints and also secured her slice of Turkey.

Turkey had been an invalid for many

long years, and its obliteration from the map of Europe was merely a question of time. These semi-civilized and blood-thirsty Turks with a hideous history drenched in innocent blood, champions of lust and rapine, oppressors of Armenia and violators of chastity, were finally driven out of Europe in 1920, hurled back once more into the dens of Asia Minor from whence they came.

Russia had long held a first mortgage upon the Turkish vagabond's estate in Europe and possessed herself of a large share of the vacated territory. But Russia, strange to relate, was kept out of Constantinople in 1999. England, Germany, and what was left of France, as well as Italy, were still fully determined that Russia should never command the Bosphorus and the Dardanelles. The European Powers were ready, as of old, to smash Russia and defeat her ambition in that direction. They knew only too well that once firmly

Shut Out of Constantinople. planted in the Ottoman capital Russia would then become the absolute master of Europe. In 1999 the Turkish territory about Constantinople, on both banks of the Bosphorus, was recognized as a neutral zone and was held in trust by the united nations of Europe. No war vessels were permitted to anchor in the Dardanelles under any pretence whatsoever.

3

CHAPTER VIII.

THE FATE OF SPAIN.

The Invention of aerial warships. In 1924 an International Congress is held at Washington. Law passed prohibiting the use of aerial warships. Spain is first to violate the compact. The penalty is extermination from the face of the earth.

SPAIN, in 1999, was reduced to a mere geographical quantity. Ever after the Spanish unpleasantness with America, in 1898, Spain's unhappy history had been sliding down a greased pole. From the moment that Columbus discovered America, Spain became a spoiled child of fortune.

In 1492 Spain had a population of 40,-000,000 people,—frugal, industrious and prosperous. In the arts and sciences they led the world in those days. In military science and navigation none could equal them. The discovery of America utterly ruined Spain in less than three hundred years. Spaniards thereafter ceased to depend upon their own energy and resources. Intoxicated by the brilliant discoveries of Columbus, the dazzling conquests of Pizarro, Cortes and De Soto, Spain has endeavored since the fifteenth century to enslave the New World and live upon the sweat of others' brows.

The acquisition of sudden and prodigious wealth in the New World ; the steady flow

The Dangers of Sudden Wealth. of money brought into Spain by slave labor ; the luxury and voluptuous ease of life thus engendered, form important factors in the history of Spain's decline. After losing all of her vast possessions in the New World, it was left to America in 1898 to give the Spaniards their coup-de-grâce and check their baggage for Madrid.

In 1942 Spain ceased to possess a government of her own. After a devastating war, (une guerre à l' outrance,) Spain ended her official existence and was parcelled out among the European nations. England, with Gibraltar to start with, secured a generous slice of the Spanish booty. In the twentieth century England was still well inclined to make the best possible use of her opportunities, and America was always glad to advance her cause, whenever it was practicable to do so.

The annihilation of Spain came about after the following manner:

In the year 1917 the world rejoiced at the prospect of a permanent solution of the war problem. The new devices invented and perfected by the deviltry of man, to be employed in the destruction of his fellow men, had reached in that year such a degree of perfection that war simply meant the wholesale destruction or total annihilation of those who engaged in it.

In 1917 aerial navigation was practically solved, and a new and vast element had **A New Element in War.** opened its possibilities to the will of man. At the close of the nineteenth century the "blue etherial" was wholly unobstructed in its vast extent and still defied the skill of our best inventors. Prof. Langley and his disciples had not yet solved the great question of ærial navigation. In 1899 this most inviting and ever tempting field of research still remained an unsolved mystery. The old fashioned balloon, with no will or control of its own, subject to the whim or caprice of every breath of air, was the best apology we could offer in 1899 for purposes of ærial navigation.

In 1917 the problem of ærial navigation had been practically solved by Tesla, in **Ærial Navigation Perfected.** whose brain many profound secrets of nature had long been harbored. With the aid and potentiality of electricity, (the slave of the twentieth century), ærial navigation had been perfected. One of the first devices invented for use in the air was the ærial warship, operated and controlled by electricity.

Loaded with a quarter ton of dynamite, these deadly warships, without anyone to navigate them could be made to hover over a city and threaten its population with total annihilation. They were popularly called "death angels." The sight of one of the warships blanched the cheeks of the most intrepid, filling the city or town over which it hovered with utmost consternation.

The human mind recoiled with horror at the thought of war with such fearful engines of destruction. **Simply Wholesale Murder.** In fact war carried on with aerial dynamite ships was no longer worthy of being called by that dignified name, it was simply a wholesale destruction of lives and property. With strange inconsistency, the world in 1917 appeared to be willing to wage war on the "retail plan." It was apparently willing to sacrifice human beings in terrible battles fought between powerfully armed vessels, with heavy rifles and rapid firing guns. The world was willing to slaughter life by one method, yet it held in abhorrence these "death angels," which accomplished a wholesale instead of a retail destruction of life and property. With an inconsistency peculiarly its own, the world in 1917 appeared quite willing that 50,000 men should be destroyed in a single battle by rapid-firing guns, which could mow down a whole regiment at a time, but the proposition to destroy an army of 50,000 men with one of the deadly aerial warships, was everywhere regarded with horror. By this decision the world placed itself in the position of a man who was willing to be killed by the shot of a six-inch rifle, yet strongly objected on the score of humanity to being riddled by the shell of a 14-inch rifle.

War at best is but a relic of barbarism, and, be it waged with ærial warships, or submarine torpedoes, with Mauser rifles or smooth bore guns, it accomplishes the same end ; nations are plunged into ruin ; the family circle is broken ; widows and orphans are left disconsolate.

Be this as it may, in the year 1924, a Congress of the leading nations was held in the city of Washington, (then situated in the State of Mexico,) and, as a result of its deliberations a solemn compact was entered into, signed by the Ambassadors of every civilized nation, and a treaty of the most binding character was ratified, in which it was stipulated that under no conditions, named or unnamed, would the use of ærial warships ever be permitted as an instrument or medium for waging war among nations.

Ærial War Ships Prohibited.

It was furthermore agreed and stipulated between these nations that if, at any future period, any nation on the habitable globe should ever permit itself to employ a system of ærial warships for the prosecution of war, the other signatories of the treaty would make common cause and combine in an attack against the offender.   They would proceed to invade its territory, destroy its cities and monuments, lay waste its plains, obliterate its flag and name from the family of nations. The remaining property of the violator of the treaty must also be seized and sold, the proceeds to be donated to charitable deeds.

It was further stipulated between the signatory powers that the punishment meted out to any violator of this solemn treaty would be in the same kind as its offending. In other words, a nation that employed the use of ærial warships and practiced the horrible system of dropping from great heights heavy charges of high explosives upon cities, fleets or shipping, would be wiped out from the face of the earth and annihilated by the same methods of destruction.

The first violator of the Washington Treaty of 1924 proved to be Spain, the

A Bad Rascal Caught. ancient home and abiding-place of the Holy Inquisition, that reprobate among nations ; the emaciated and wasted offspring of priestcraft. To her in 1930 was meted out the condign punishment which she richly deserved for her flagrant violation of the Washington Treaty in prosecuting her war against Morocco. During this war, in the year 1929, Spain had resorted to the use of ærial warships and by employing a fleet of "death angels," she had utterly destroyed the

ancient city of Fez, the capital of that barbaric North African State, reducing the city
into a heap of ruins and causing the slaughter, in less than thirty minutes, of over
175,000 people.   Tangier, on the northern
boundary of Morocco, a city of 75,000 population, had also suffered the same fate from
the Spanish "death angels." Tangier, with
its inhabitants, was reduced to ashes in less
than ten minutes.

In order to chastise Spain for her wanton
cruelty and open violation of the international convention of 1924, a peremptory
note was served upon the Madrid authorities, signed by the Treaty Powers, with the
names of America and England at the head
of the list.   It was particularly observed
that the signature of the United States of
the Americas was underscored, as though to
remind Spain that America had not forgotten the wrongs of Cuba.

On the 21st day of April, 1930, (just
thirty-two years after the declaration of our
first war with Spain,) no-
Hoisting   tice was served upon the
the   Madrid authorities that
Storm-signal. within thirty days from
date, the allied nations of the world would
mobilize their ærial war fleets and proceed to
devastate Spanish territory.   This ultimatum included Ceuta, the Balearic islands,
as well as the ever-faithful isles of the Can-
aries.

This international ultimatum was dispatched in conformity to the terms of the Washington Treaty of 1924, which demanded, irrevocably and without appeal, the extinction of any nation that employed such barbarous methods of warfare as ærial warships and the practice of hurling gun-cotton, dynamite and nitro-glycerine from the skies upon defenceless cities.

At last Spanish pride was humbled. With a terrible doom to face, with no friend to counsel, succor or comfort her, Spain was at last brought to the dregs of humiliation. In vain did that unhappy country plead for leniency and mercy. Spain was willing to sue for peace and safety upon any terms, but in vain did that stricken nation wave the olive branch.

Spain Sheds Crocodile Tears.

The countenance of the world was withdrawn from Spain. The Treaty Powers were obdurate and Spain must suffer for the terrible slaughter of Fez and Tangier. The world in 1930 demanded that an example should be made. It was determined to settle, once and forever, the important question of using dynamite and other fulminants as a weapon of war thrown down from airships. It had been determined that any nation employing such barbarous methods of warfare should be uprooted from the face of the earth.

The object and purpose of the thirty-day notice was to allow the entire population, men, women and children, ample time to leave the doomed kingdom. The Treaty

Thirty Days to Leave Spain. Powers, in seeking to punish Spain, did not wish to sacrifice life. The punishment Spain was to receive consisted in the annihilation of her kingdom and the destruction of her cities and monuments. Like modern Jews, who had lost their Palestine, they were thereafter to be scattered over the face of the globe, with no country and no national ensign of their own. Such was the fiat of the nations in 1930 and this decree was fulfilled to the letter.

CHAPTER IX.

THE ANNIHILATION OF SPAIN.

Arrival of the "Death Angels" over Spain. Spaniards cross the Pyrenees into France. The doom of Weyler and his cohorts. "Remember the Maine." Madrid and the principal cities of Spain in ashes. Portugal's action applauded. No more aerial warships.

ON the 21st day of May, 1930, a remarkable sight presented itself over the Pyrenean range of mountains on the northern boundary of Spain, dividing that country from her northerly neighbor, "la belle France." High above the peaks of **Arrival of the " Death Angels."** that natural barrier between those two countries, and visible to the naked eye, could be seen what appeared to be a large flock of birds of enormous size, moving swiftly and silently in a southerly direction.

Vast multitudes of Spaniards who were crossing the Pyrenees to seek shelter in French territory, gazed with awe upon the ominous sight presented by these "death angels" as they proceeded south on their errand of destruction. They knew only too well the character of these deadly messengers of war whose use had been prohibited in battle by all civilized nations. In the case of Spain they were not used for purposes of warfare but merely as instruments of punishment for her wanton violation of the Treaty.

During the preceding thirty days the volume of immigration from Spain into France had kept an unbroken stream. On the 21st day of May, 1930, the appointed day of doom, a large share of the Spanish population had found its way across the border into France, and some of the provinces about Madrid, notably Segovia, Castille and Salamanca, were as innocent of population as the desert of Sahara is of cascades.

On that memorable day of May, 1930, the cities of Spain might easily have been

Spanish Cities Two For a Cent. bought up for a song or a jack lantern. Weyler and his ferocious cutthroats, (the same imps who blew up our Maine and martyred 266 brave American sailors), were the only beings who remained in Spain on that day of doom. The gang had the run of the kingdom for a few brief hours and were probably amusing themselves very much after the manner of rats who enjoy the exclusive privilege of a sinking ship.

The Butcher and his satellites were holding high carnival in the regal apartments of the Royal Palace in doomed Madrid, when the ærial war craft of America, England and the Allied nations, silently stood guard and floated over the city, veritable angels of death, fearful to behold.

The cellars of the Royal Palace had been ransacked and wines of the choicest vintage

Handwriting on the Wall. were being guzzled by the Weyler brigands. Amidst revelry a n d shouting, and the din of rattling castenets, the mazes of fandangos were performed by voluptuous and sinuous Castillian sirens, from whose wild eyes blazed forth that baleful light, incited by wine and unholy passion. These dark, olive-skin belles in their terpsichores before the Butcher and his aides, were as innocent of habiliments as Madame Eve when that exalted personage made her début in Eden. In the midst of this debauchery, and while revelry was yet at its zenith, history again repeated itself. Suddenly, like a prolonged flash of lightning, the revelers saw distinctly the handwriting on the wall. It was an inscription that carried terror and consternation into the hearts of the Weylerites and read : " Remember the Maine."

At this critical and interesting part of the program, Capt. Sigsbee, (then eighty-one years of age,) who in 1930 commanded the ærial warship "Maine," and who had been especially selected for that mission, gave the signal and from her kelson the ærial " Maine" dropped a little surprise package containing one hundred and thirty pounds of dynamite upon the Royal Palace of Spain. Weyler and his gang, one moment later, were roasting in company with their forefathers. Such, then, was the fate of Weyler, the destroyer of our noble "Maine," an

**More
Spanish Mules
Killed.**

arch fiend whose cruel orders were blindly obeyed by others of his ilk, carrying to unhappy Cuba a degree of misery, starvation and death that shocked the entire world.

The British ærial warships, as well as those of Germany, Russia, Austria, Italy, France, Holland, Greece and Japan, took their signal from the first shot or discharge of dynamite dropped by the "Maine," and joined forces with the American ærial warships in the total annihilation of Madrid. The scene of destruction that followed the attack of these ærial warships baffles all belief. Indeed, naught may come within the scope of human imagination that can depict the horrors, wholesale slaughter and utter desolation that may be wrought by ærial warships. Ships floating in the air

**It's Murder
in
The Air.**

two miles over a city and dropping within its limits huge charges of dynamite, are fearful engines of destruction. In the twinkle of an eye they can turn stately churches, lofty buildings, beautiful homes, hospitals, colleges, parks and pleasure resorts into ashes, and still vastly more terrible would be the loss of life.

The bare thought that human beings with souls to save and a God to answer to, might,

THE DESTRUCTION OF MADRID IN 1930.

in a flash, be hurled into eternity by these
ærial dynamite ships, without a moment's
warning, and their habitations turned into
charnel-houses, is in itself sufficient to make
one's flesh creep.

The Washington treaty of 1924, forbid-
ding forever the use of this barbarous
method of warfare and threatening with destruction any nation that employed it, was
a wise and humane compact.

Spain's flagrant violation of the international treaty in 1929, when she wantonly
destroyed Fez and Tangier, was universally
condemned. On the other hand, the destruction and razing of Spain in 1930, as a
punishment for her bad faith, received the
warmest commendations of the world. It
was fully realized that Spain's chastisement
fitted her case as perfectly as the bark fits
the tree that it encircles.

Yet, the razing of Spain in 1930 fills
one's better nature with sadness. The
Too Bad about Spain. widespread destruction
of a kingdom replete
with historic memories,
rich in treasure-troves of
art and science, dotted with thriving cities,
fertile plains, lovely vales and teeming with
beautiful homes, appeals to heart, as well
as imagination. Although richly meriting
her fate in 1930, Spain's doom in that year
deeply stirred the hearts of all humanity,
but the lesson it taught was that the world
would never tolerate the use in war of

ærial dynamite warships, and this lesson proved a salutary one.

From Cadiz to Saragossa, and from Alicante to Corunna, the deadly ærial ships pressed on their way, sweeping destruction before them.   The chief cities of Spain, namely, Barcelona, Valencia, Seville, Malaga, Murcia, Cartagena, Granada, Cadiz and Saragossa, were all destroyed in rapid succession, after the fate of Madrid had been decided.   The costly palaces of the Madrid grandees crumbled into dust from only a few dynamite discharges of these air-ships.

Sad indeed it was to witness the destruction of the magnificent paintings in the Royal Art Gallery of Madrid, containing as it did in 1930 three thousand chef-d'œuvres of the world's immortal artists.   The gallery contained the best examples of Titian, Raphael, Rubens, Muerillo, Van Dyck, Veronese and Tenier, a grand collection of rare paintings that were valued at $300,-000,000, and that had required several hundreds of years to collect.

Strange to say, in 1930, there was no cathedral in Madrid for the air-ships to destroy.   For some reason, unknown even to Spaniards, their national capital had never enjoyed this luxury.   It is a maxim, old as the hills, that shoemakers are usually the ones who wear the shabbiest shoes ; the ill-dressed man in a community is very apt to be the tailor ; the most neglected man during sickness is oftentimes the physician, and the man who invariably neglects to make his will is the lawyer. Following in the line of this well-established rule, it ceases to be a surprise that priest-ridden Spain, the first-born of Rome, should find herself without a cathedral within the limits of her national capital. If the cathedral of Madrid escaped the palsied touch of the dynamite air-ships the reason therefor was simple enough. Madrid never possessed one.

Portugal escaped the ravages of the dynamite air-ships, and in 1999 that kingdom **Ordered West by Portugal.** still proudly guarded the western shores of the Iberian peninsula. In the spring of the year 1898, Portugal endeared herself to every American heart when her government ordered Admiral Cervera and his squadron to sail away from her possessions, the Cape de Verde islands, and "go west." Cervera had to face the music, and it was with heavy hearts that the mariners on board of the Oquendo, Marie de Teresa, Vizcaya, Colon, and the torpedo destroyers, Pluton and Furore, weighed anchor and, like Columbus, set their faces toward the Western Hemisphere, but, this time, with the certainty that their noble vessels never again would plough their prows in European waters.

The inglorious fate of Spain in 1930 ever after proved a warning to all other nations. In 1999 air-ships navigated the "blue

ethereal " in every quarter of the globe.
It was a safe, economical and swift method

**No More
Ærial
Warships.**

of transportation, but after the destruction of
Spain, in 1930, ærial warships were put out of com-
mission and condemned.   In 1999 so strin-
gent were the international laws against
their use that the mere possession of an
ærial warship by any nation was likely to
embroil others in a war of extermination
and on suspicion alone a most rigid investi-
gation was instituted.

CHAPTER X.

EUROPE IN 1999.

The Pope Casts his Lot in the New World.   Complications in Europe Rendered his Residence in Rome Undesirable.   No Refuge in Europe Available for his Holiness.   Generous Offer of the Southern States of the American Union.   The Papal See transferred to Rio Janeiro in 1945.

THE relations of the United States of the Americas with Italy in 1999 were of a character that demand more than a passing notice, going far to illustrate the political eminence that had been attained in that year by the great American Republic.

In the year 1927, the long standing and severe tension that had existed between the Papacy and the Italian government ever since Napoleon III in 1870 withdrew his French garrison from the Holy City, became greatly intensified and had reached an acute stage that proved beyond human endurance.

The strained relations between the Vatican and the Quirinal had reached a critical stage.   The fierce struggle between Church and State had attained a point of utmost tension.   It became obvious, even in that year, that the break and parting of the ways could not be very distant.   In 1927 the Popes of Rome had already been prisoners in the palace of the Vatican for a

period of over fifty years.   Patience in their
case had ceased to be a virtue.   Rome had
long been a house divided against itself and
its rule under two kings could not always
endure.   The delicate position of the Pope
became a most unenviable one.   The inso-
lence of the Roman rabble even found its
way under the glorious dome of St. Peter,
where, on Palm Sunday, in the year 1923
Pope Pius X was insulted by a clique from
the Roman slums.   That the Holy Pontiff,
the spiritual ruler and sovereign of 328,000,
000 Catholics, should experience insult in
St. Peter's, his citadel of strength and
power, proved a scandal beyond belief.

Convinced that his temporal power was
forever broken, Pope Leo XIV in the year

**The Pope
Decides
to Leave.**

1945 decided, after con-
sulting a Conclave of
Cardinals, to abandon
the city of Romulus and
Remus and to shake from his sandals the
dust of ancient Rome.   It was at first
thought that the College of Cardinals would
check their baggage and take the overland
route to Avignon, in southern France, an
honor which many centuries before had
already fallen to the lot of that ancient
municipality.

But it was otherwise decreed and
great was the astonishment of the world
when its nerves were thoroughly startled
by the startling news that Pope Leo XIV
had elected to remove the Papal See

from Rome and to establish it in the
United States of the Americas. The
world's astonishment was akin to consternation when the news of this radical
change of base was first announced and it
was learned that the Vatican intended to
cast its lot in the new world.

A proposition to transplant the Papal See
from its ancient anchorage in the Italian

**It Startles
One's
Nerves.**

peninsula into the new
world would have been
scouted in 1899 with
scorn and derision as the
wild phantasy of a babbling maniac. People
living in 1899 might perhaps have seriously
entertained a proposition to remove the
pyramids of Egypt from their ancient
foundations and transfer them to the sand-
lots of San Francisco, to open up a Chinese
laundry in the King's Chamber ; a proposition to dispatch an army of laborers with
shovels to the crater of Vesuvius and attempt to extinguish that volcano by shovel-
ing in sand, might, in 1899, have been regarded as a plausible undertaking ; the attempt of a delegation of Protestant minis-
ters to personally convert the Sultan of
Turkey from Mohamedanism and induce
him to attend a camp-meeting, might have
commended itself to all good citizens in
1899, but the startling proposition to remove the Papal Court from ancient Rome
to South America, appeared to all minds in
1899 as the most improbable of all improba-

bilities, yet in 1945, (forty-six years later,)
the public mind was better prepared for this
great change and the removal of the Court
of Rome in that year to Rio Janeiro was
entertained in better grace and in a more
conciliatory spirit.

In 1945 the position of the Papacy in
Rome was no longer endurable.   The

**Rome Unsafe
for
the Pontiff.**

sacred person of the
Pontiff became no longer
safe within the precincts
of the Eternal City.
The Vatican had been frequently violated
by mobs from the banks of the Tiber and
the slums of Rome, over which the Italian
government could effect no control.   The
revered head of the church, like his Divine
Master while on earth, knew not where to
lay his head.

Europe in 1945 had no refuge or shelter
to offer to His Holiness.   Russia, the home
of the Greek church, could offer him no
asylum, where one of his exalted rank
might dwell in peace.   Austria, that stead-
fast and ever faithful son of the church,
would gladly have sheltered the Papal
Court, assuring it permanent safety and a
splendor commensurate with its prestige, but,
unfortunately for Austria in 1945 that
country was rent in twain, a shadow of its
former greatness.   Hungary had long enjoyed her richly merited independence and
in that year had become a leading European
power.

The eyes of the Papacy could not turn
to Spain for succor in 1945.   Spain in that
year was reduced to a barren waste, having
expiated her crime of 1930, that of employing powerful fulminants from air-ships
to destroy two African cities.   France in
1945 had no refuge to offer the Pope   As
a result of two unfortunate wars, she had
passed into the custody of Germany, occupying the position of a mere vassal.

Realizing the serious difficulties which
environed the Papal See in 1945, the
Catholic states of the southern tier of
the United States of the Americas,
known as South America, made an urgent
appeal that the Court of Rome might be
removed into their midst.

Colombia, Ecuador, Bolivia, Chile, Peru,
Venezuela, Brazil, Uruguay, Argentina,
The South to the Rescue. Paragua and Patagonia
levied contributions
among the faithful and
between them the muni-
ficient sum of $500,000,000 was raised, to
be placed at the disposal of the Pope.
Accompanying this gift offering was sent
an earnest petition and prayer that the
Pope would consent to abide in the new
world, where a splendid reservation consisting of 17,000 square miles of choice
lands had been placed at his disposal in the
neighborhood of Rio Janeiro.

In the petition of the South American
States praying His Holiness to acquiesce in

this important project, it was pointed out
that the Pope would be domiciled upon the
only continent which was catholic in its entirety, with no creed to oppose, and, in removing the throne of St. Peter to Rio
Janeiro, the Pope would occupy the position
of a patriarch surrounded by his faithful
children. The invisible, but none the less
galling fetters, that had enslaved the Pope
since 1870, making him virtually a prisoner
in the Vatican, would be entirely removed.
In the State of Brazil he might rule a
principality of no mean proportions, far
larger and immeasurably more wealthy than
the Papal kingdom of 1870 when Pius IX
was yet King of Rome. The catholic citizens of South America represented fully the
many advantages of removing the Papal
Court from the old into the new world.

It will be recollected that in 1999 the
total population of the United States of the
Americas amounted to 531,000,000. Of
this vast population at least 175,000,000
citizens residing in South America were ad-
herents of the church of Rome.

The liberal offer that came from the
South American States received the utmost

**The Pope
Accepts
the Offer.**

attention from the Papal
authorities. To with-
draw from that ancient
city seemed like the up ·
rooting of all traditions. The irreligious
were prone to make merry over the proposition, predicting with strange irreverence,

that in Rio Janeiro the Pope would feel like
a cat in a strange garret. But with such
innuendoes we have nothing in common.
Let history proceed undisturbed in its course.

It required a heroic sacrifice to give up
Rome, filled with the most precious historic
memories, a city in which lies enshrined
the dust of St. Peter's successors. This
step meant the abandonment of that magnificent cathedral, which in 1999 still
formed an aureole of glory about the Eternal City. But Rome in 1945 was no longer
a safe tabernacle for the Papacy. Its mobs
were unbridled in their license. The person of the Pontiff was no longer safe within
the walls of the Vatican. The Italian
government proved to be an abettor,
if not an instigator, of these outrages.

With a dark, threatening cloud hovering
over the throne of St. Peter in Europe, and

**All Headed
for
the West.**
on the other hand, bright
skies and a most alluring
and tempting prospect
eagerly awaiting its
transferment to Rio de Janeiro, after long
hestitation and endless Conclaves, the
Sacred College of Cardinals. (the Pope con-
curring,) gave its official sanction in 1945
to the removal of the Papal See to the
Western Hemisphere, under the ægis of
the great American Constitution, the noblest
document ever written by the fallible pen of
man, a charter which protects and defends
all who are worthy and they who seek its
sheltering folds. 4

CHAPTER XI.

ENGLAND'S DOMAIN IN 1999.

England Rules Supreme in Africa in 1999. Electric Railroads Built by American Engineers Cover the Dark Continent. France Suffers Two Waterloos. England's Rule in India Unshaken in the Twentieth Century.

IN 1999 England was the ruler of Africa and her domain over the Dark Continent was indisputable. From the Delta of the Nile to Cape Town, from Abyssinia to Liberia, the British lion was free to roam and roar throughout the enormous, heart-shaped African continent. From Alexandria to Cape Town became, in 1999, a comparatively short journey over the electric railroads which in that year traversed the entire length of the Nile basin, with important stations at Berber and Khartoum, Uganda, Zambo to Pretoria, thence to the Terminal of the roads at Cape Town. This electric railroad through the Nile basin, the lake regions and heart of the African continent, was completed and in operation in 1930, after a sacrifice in its construction of 19,000 lives and an outlay of $152,000,000. It proved to be, however, the backbone of Africa, the vertebral column from which scores of other electric railroad branches

It Reduced the Census.

THE BEST OF FRIENDS.

reached out both east and west, like the ribs of a mastodon.

The great presiding genius and leading spirit in African railroads was Cecil Rhodes, the same who was regarded as being the most prominent colonial Englishman. It was through his perseverance and untiring energy that the great system of African railroads was created in 1930. Rhodes was a really great man. Thousands courted his favor and smile, and tens of thousands trembled at his frown. Throughout Southern Africa so great in 1899 was his power and influence that he was called the "Deputy Almighty."

In the construction of these African electric railroads America played an important rôle. Cecil Rhodes was at first inclined to award the contracts for rails, copper wires, cars and general equipment to English manufacturing firms but his worthy patriotic sentiments soon vanished when it was demonstrated clear as sunlight, even early as 1898 that America could produce a far superior grade of machinery in much less time and at much less cost. In 1901 Cecil Rhodes awarded all his heavy contracts to American firms. In other words, England furnished the capital and America practically built the entire system of African railroads in 1930.

The first "eye opener" in the line of American competition against British machinery came into prominence in the spring of 1899, when work had already commenced on the north division of the great trunk line through Africa. The Atbara bridge and the first lesson in industrial economy that it taught, will not soon be forgotten. Bids were invited from British and American bridge builders in April, 1899. It was represented to all competitors that the proposed bridge must be completed in the shortest time possible.

America Leads the World.

When the bids were opened it was discovered that the English engineers required seven months to complete the work, while their American competitors guaranteed to complete and deliver the bridge in forty-two days from date of signing the contract and the work was to be completed for a much less sum than the price demanded by the English builders.

The lesson of the Atbara bridge was not lost upon the great " Deputy Almighty " of South Africa and Cecil Rhodes became the means during the first quarter of the twentieth century of securing many million dollars to the American trade. Africa's most urgent needs in 1900 were railroads and missionaries. England supplied a very superior article of the latter, while in the railroad field no country could equal the American output.

A Peaceful Victory.

In the nineteenth century it had been the unpleasant experience of France to suffer at the hands of England two Waterloos. One was the great and only Waterloo, which drenched the soil of Belgium with the blood of many brave men. Waterloo, Jr., overtook the French soldiers at Fashoda, on Africa's soil in 1899. When in that year England ordered France to leave Fashoda without any further ceremony a victory was won by England, bloodless, but none the less effective.

France Eats "Humble Pie."

After the Fashoda incident France gradually lost her African provinces, leaving England in undisputed sway over a continent that in wealth and resources proved far superior to her great Indian Empire. In 1999 Alexander II, of Great Britain, ruled over a mighty empire. In the nineteenth century British kings and queens were just plain, every day royalties, transacting a legitimate business in that line and otherwise enjoying the respect and confidence of their patrons. It was generally understood that the "king can do no wrong." This was indisputable for the simple reason they never did anything at all. But when great Africa became a British province, it was then felt necessary to add still another title to the British Crown and in 1999 Britain's Sovereign became known to his chums and acquaintances as King of Great Britain and

Ireland, D. F., Emperor of India, Mogul
of Africa and Right Bower of the Americas,
because, in 1999 none of England's important deals were regarded as complete without a Yankee plum in the pie.　　Sometimes England contrived, as the phrase
goes, to "get her foot in it" but cousin
Jonathan across the salt pond, always man-
aged to yank her out.

In 1999 England still held a firm grip upon India.　The secret of Samson's herculean strength was due to
the fact that a lawn-mow-
er had never tampered
with his hair.　But the
secret of the British lion's power in India
did not consist in the fact that the lordly
beast cultivated a full mane.

**How England
Holds
India.**

India in 1999, as in the year 1899, still
continued to remain the world's most brilliant illustration that nations which are divided among themselves must inevitably
fall.　In 1899 the question was repeatedly
asked, how can England with a mere corporal's guard, hold together the vast, mystic
India under her sway ?　How can a nation
of 40,000,000 people, like England, hold
under her sway a far distant continent like
India with its population of 350,000,000
people ?

In 1999 India still remained a house divided against itself and England was boss
of the whole ranch.　The eighty different
principalities of India, each one speaking

a different dialect and governed by alien potentates, fired by mutual hatreds which were fanned by fierce jealousies and the immutable laws of caste, were still as far apart in 1999, in point of harmony and cohesive action, as the Himalayan peaks are remote from the spice groves of Ceylon.

Cannot Hold Together. If at any period in the eighteenth, nineteenth or twentieth centuries these principalities of India could have united themselves together in a common cause and arisen in the might of their power against British rule, England would be driven out of India in ten days' time. India's 350,000,000 population represents an enormous mass, but, as long as it remains divided into practically eighty different nations, all of them animated by bitter hatreds and antagonisms, England will experience no trouble in retaining absolute control of her large but very acrimonious Indian family.

The power and stamina of the Anglo-Saxon race, which already dominated the **Anglo-Saxons Rule the World.** world in 1999 through the vast Republic of the Americas and the worldwide British Empire, exemplified itself in a high degree in the British government of India. Only one desperate struggle was ever attempted against British rule in India and the disastrous failure of the mutiny in 1857 was yet fresh in the minds of many in 1999.

The great, mighty India, the home of mysteries that baffle all reason ; the fount which holds the sacred Ganges and boasts of Benares' holy soil, was still under the lion's paw in 1999 and bid fair to remain under British rule for many centuries yet to come. Mystic India, the land of the loftiest mountains, deepest jungles and broadest plains ; the home of Pharsee and Thug ; the lair of lion, tiger, leopard and elephant ; the Eden of the deadly cobra, India, the world's vast and mystic continent, remained a British province throughout the twentieth century.

CHAPTER XII.

BACK IN GOD'S COUNTRY AGAIN.

A Grand Constitution that could Govern the World. The American Flag must Rule the Western Hemisphere and None Save God can Prevent this. America's Perilous Over-confidence. Our Great Navy in 1999. England's Friendly Offices in 1898. America and Great Britain Firm Friends Forevermore.

HAVING thus briefly reviewed the condition of Europe in 1999; the changes that had been effected in the map of that continent ; the cordial relations existing between the American Eagle and the British Lion in that year ; the acknowledged supremacy of America and England over the entire world ; the obliteration of Spain in 1930 ; the fall of France in 1935 ; the banishment of moslem rule from Europe and the grandeur of British rule in Africa and India, let us again return to God's own country, *The United States of the Americas*, which chosen land, in 1999, became the wealthiest, most prosperous and powerful of all nations upon this inhabitable globe. Having traveled abroad in the preceding chapter to secure a glimpse of the world's condition in that year, we gladly set foot again in the new world to examine more closely and accurately into the status of the great American Colossus.

If there are any who believe that the great and infallible constitution of the

It Could Govern the World. United States of America is not broad and strong enough to include in its scope and government every country in our Western Hemisphere from Alaska to Patagonia ; if there are any Americans who believe that Central and South American Republics can never be governed under our American Republic, employing the same language and the same coinage, all sheltered under the noble flag of Bunker Hill, to such unbelievers in the future expansion of America we appeal in vain through these pages. They fail to understand that America has a great duty to perform and is destined to become the light of the world.

To any fair minded and candid student of history the conclusion must come with force that America with

It is the Hand of Destiny. her forty-five states in 1899 was a mere local affair compared with the certainty of all the other republics joining under one government with ours in 1999.

America in 1899 was yet in the cradle of her infancy, occupying a modest and narrow strip of territory extending from Maine to Florida ; fringed by Canada on the north and laved by the waters of the Mexican gulf on the south.

Her position on this continent was that of a Gulliver by whose side the other southern republics looked like Liliputians. Providing that the giant is gifted not only with strength and a stout heart, but governed, also, by good principles, why should the Liliputian Republics of Central and South America fear? Would it not be better for them to make common cause with their great American neighbor and live under one flag?

In 1899 the tendency of the period was to consolidate; the "trust epidemic" then **Uncle Sam's Big Trust.** raged at its height; the aim of that period, at least in commercial affairs, was to gather together the small concerns and unite them into a whole. *The United States of the Americas* in 1999 was largely built on the trust principle. Uncle Sam was running the biggest concern in the government line and the little South American Republics had simply been gathered in by the big fellow. They all were merged into one great American nation, governed by the same constitution, and all lifted up their gaze with patriotic pride to the Stars and Stripes.

At this juncture it might be interesting to learn by what means and in what manner was this vast American Republic protected by sea and land in 1999. Conscious of her vast resources and enormous strength, America from the close of the Civil War in

1865 to the year 1885 remained practically
unarmed, keeping on hand a mere corporal's guard in the shape of an army.   Her
navy up to 1882 consisted of an aggregation
of warships of more or less antiquity, mere
washtubs with smooth bore guns, whose
ordnance, discharged against a modern
battleship, would have about the same
effect as throwing boiled peas at a brick
wall.

Twenty years after the close of the Civil
War, in 1885, America had commenced to
Uncle Sam Wakes Up. rub her eyes and to
awaken from her peril-
ous Rip Van Winkle
siesta of two decades
and to realize, at last, that a strong navy
had become a national necessity.   Over ·
confidence is a dangerous foe to national
safety.   America, a land filled with liberty-
loving patriots and master mechanics, set
to work none too soon to provide herself
with a navy; fighting machines that in point
of speed and prowess would compare favorably with the output of the best foreign
shipyards.   It became obvious to the veri-
est child that if our national dignity at
home or abroad were to be maintained, and,
if we did not proposed to be bluffed by small
concerns like Chile and Spain, the best
thing to do about a navy would be to build
it at once, forthwith, "and on the word
go."

Congress took spirited action in the mat-

ter, making liberal appropriations for the
construction of a first grade fleet of modern
warships, armed and equipped with best
and most penetrating rifles.   This patriotic
and sensible policy had been inaugurated
none too soon.

The month of January, 1898, found
America in possession of a small, but highly

**Small
but
Powerful.**

efficient navy and on the
brink of war.   What we
had in the line of war
vessels was of the best,
but America could proudly boast of something immeasurably better than a few fine
ships and heavy guns.   We possessed what
no Congress or Parliament could make to
order or purchase by appropriation, and
that was a keen, patriotic sentiment
throughout both the American army and
navy.

" The man behind the gun," anxious to
lay down his life by the side of the power-

**The True
American
Hero.**

ful breech-loading de-
stroyer he loved so well
to train and groom; "the
man behind the gun"
who loved and cared for his mighty weapon as a father would his child ; watching
it by night and day, praying for the hour
when he might belch from its throat missiles
of destruction into the enemy's ranks,—
" the man behind the gun," God bless him,
is America's own true born.   In the hour of
peril, at Manila, Santiago and at Puerto

Rico, these heroes, man and gun, did their duty right nobly and well.   In 1999 the world still rang with the valor of their deeds.

But America in 1898 found herself still unprepared.   The war issue was lodged with a power of the third magnitude.   Left alone with the Dons the tale would soon be told.   Only one year before our war with the yellow and red flag, an American gentleman summed up the situation in a very concise manner :   '' When we get at the Spaniards, they'll hold together just long enough to get kicked to pieces.''

But Spain had other partners, two powerful nations, who, for selfish reasons, would have been only too glad to give Uncle Sam a punch in the ribs. Germany, having been fortified by a bribe from Spain for her co-operation against America, having been promised by Spain as a reward for assistance the entire group of the Philippines, was only too eager to close the bargain.   The Teutons were spoiling for a fight with Uncle Sam, ostensibly in behalf of Spain, but more especially for a grab at the Philippines.   France, on the other hand, distinctly recollected that she owned and held the bulk of Spanish securities and if the Dons in their brush with America took ''a header,'' these Spanish securities would not be worth a last year's bird nest.   And now comes an important question :   Was America prepared in 1899 to clash in naval combat with the combined forces of Spain, France and Germany? Josh Billings would have made short shift of his reply by saying : " Well, hardly."

Spain's two unhappy partners, in their dilemma then turned their eyes and steps

Called at the Captain's Office.

toward a little island that lies slightly north of their territory. France and Germany heard the growl of the British Lion and before they joined Spain in a war against America, John Bull must be consulted. As a result of their interview this ill-mated pair became well convinced that England would put up with none of their nonsense and would not remain neutral should they join Spain in hostilities against America. France and Germany became converted to other views and very wisely decided to remain at home, meek as lambs, while Uncle Sam was carving up Spain to suit the queen's taste.

In 1999 our American patriots did not propose to get caught in the trap of January, 1898, in which America found herself. In the year first named America was able to meet in war any combination of European nations that might hazard themselves in the field against her. The unfortunate spectacle of a great nation like America, on the eve of war, rushing around as we certainly did in March, 1898, buying up odds and ends of war vessels and fairly begging to buy smokeless powder at any price, will never again be repeated in this great country. The lesson of 1898 was yet fresh in the minds of all in 1999. Americans of the twentieth century were too shrewd to get caught napping again in that manner.

In 1999 the United States of the Americas embraced eighty-five states. Canada

The New American Navy. had been divided into two American States, namely, East and West Canada. The original territory of the United States in that year consisted of sixty-two sovereign states ; Texas alone had been divided into three separate states. To these were added the six states of Central America, namely, the newly created American States of Mexico, Nicaragua, Salvador, Costo Rica, Guatemala and Honduras. Next came the newly admitted American States of Colombia, Venezuela, Ecuador, Bolivia, Brazil, Peru, Chile, Argentine, Uruguay, Paraguay and Patagonia, making a grand total of eighty-five states, which formed in 1999 the United States of the Americas.

By enactment of Congress provision had been made that every State in the Union must build, equip and maintain at its own cost at least one battleship of the most modern type and unrivalled power ; one armored cruiser of the highest speed, (35 knots per hour,) and three submarine destroyers of the most approved pattern and of the most enterprising character.

As a result of this wise policy the navy
of the Americas in 1999 consisted of eighty-
five (85) first grade battleships ; one hundred and seventy (170) of the swiftest and
most powerful cruisers ; two hundred and

**Five hundred
and Ten
Warships.**

fifty-five (255) submarine
destroyers, p o p u l a r l y
called in that year, "up-
lifters." Such was the
numerical strength of the American Navy
during the closing period of the twentieth
century, on a peace footing.   In the remote
possibility of a war, provision had been
made to mobilize the American fleet upon
a far more formidable standard of efficiency.
The total number of our war craft of all
classes aggregated in that year, five hundred and ten (510) vessels.

When one reflects that the coast-line of
the great Republic, along the Atlantic and
Pacific shores of the Americas, embraces
fully 34,000 miles, every mile of which was
entitled to our national defence, it will be
recognized that the American Navy in 1999
was barely in keeping with the vast proportions of the Republic it had been created to
defend.   Indeed, it was regarded as being a
modest establishment of its kind, judged by
the standards of that period.

The question very properly offers itself,
"If the United States of the Americas in
1999 represented such a powerful nation,
wealthy and prosperous, potent in enterprise and industry, what use had it for a

navy of five hundred and ten warships ? "
This question is easily answered by quoting
an old and sterling axiom : '' In time of
peace we must prepare for war."

The folly of March 1898, when America,
on the eve of war with Spain, rushed in

**Not to be
Caught
Again.**

breathless haste i n t o
every European navy-
yard to purchase any
thing that could float a
gun, and offered haystacks of gold for
smokeless powder, was not to be repeated
in 1999.   It was recognized in that year
that the best guarantee for peace was to
maintain an efficient army and powerful
navy, to exact a proper respect for a flag
that protected 531,000,000 American citizens.

The big American Republic in 1999 did
not propose to place itself, with its vast
population and interminable coast-line, in
the humiliating condition of China, a people who, though mighty in population, remain helpless as infants in matters of
national defence.   America did not intend
to suffer the fate of China.   Although her
territory was vast and her population
reckoned by the half-billion, America did
not propose to permit European cormorants
to pounce upon her coasts, and, as in the
case of China, steal a whole country under the guise of civilizing it.   In 1999 the
Americas maintained a formidable army and
navy in order to impress the fact upon the

world that we were not like lambs, wholly without means of self-defense.

The perilous American policy, inaugurated after the Civil War, of existing without any army or navy worthy of the name, was exposed through our war with Spain. Americans cheerfully acknowledged the fact that England's friendliness tended to bring that war to an early close. Even Spain in 1898 professed to hold our army in exalted contempt, regarding Americans as a nation wholly unfit for war, at best, a nation of wheat raisers and pork-packers. Many Spaniards honestly imagined that Admiral Cervera could sail his squadron into New York harbor, land his marines at Coney Island and after bombarding the clams and battling with lager kegs, march his men over the Brooklyn Bridge and capture City Hall.

In 1999 Americans did not propose to again get caught napping, as in the "good old **Eternal Vigilance in 1999.** days" of 1898. They remained armed and ready for war on drop of the hat. No nation in the former year would venture unaided to combat the great American Republic. America in the twentieth century became invincible.

CHAPTER XIII.

Our Army and Navy in 1999.

Justice done to both Schley and Sampson. The American victory off Santiago opens the eyes of the world. Emperor Wilhelm congratulates himself. America maintains a vigorous Monroe Doctrine.

LONG before the advent of 1910 every trace of the bitter controversy that had so long disturbed American naval circles over the Sampson-Schley quarrel, had fortunately been effaced. The hatchet had been buried, or figuratively speaking, had been thrown overboard, and in 1999 this unhappy feud, which tarnished the prestige of the world's foremost navy, had been obliterated. In 1999, when all heat or vestige of passion had passed away, this unfortunate episode was regarded as being the one and only blot that associated itself with the memory of a wonderful naval exploit, the brilliant engagement on that ever memorable Sunday morning of July 3, 1898, when the Spanish squadron steamed into the jaws of death.

Time accomplishes wonders. It tones down the angles; it dulls the keenest edge and can even render mild, bitter animosities, which, alas, often sting sharper than serpent fangs.

The Brave American Officers.

Long before 1900 it was universally acknowledged that gallant Admiral Schley had been persecuted. His tormentors, men of high station, became heartily ashamed of persecuting a brave officer who had committed what apparently, in their judgment, appeared to be the crime of annihilating the Spanish squadron off Santiago.

Students of history in 1910 very naturally asked themselves : "If Admiral Schley was so bitterly assailed at the close of a sweeping victory, in what manner would he have been treated by these carping critics had a portion of Cervera's fleet made good its escape ?"

Admiral Sampson appeared to be willing

Sampson's Unlucky Absence.

and anxious to secure credit for a victory that had been fought and won during his absence. But the question arises, would Admiral Sampson have been willing to shoulder the blame if Cervera's vessels had escaped destruction or would he have saddled Admiral Schley with the responsibility ? The reader must form his own conclusions in this matter. On the other hand, all impartial students of history in the twentieth century cheerfully accorded to Admiral Sampson full credit for his gallant services on blockade duty during that war. His responsibilities were great and pressing, and he discharged his duties with utmost fidelity.

A pathetic story indeed is that of the "Man in the Iron Mask." None can read that page of French history without being touched by the sad fate of this mysterious prisoner of state, who was generally supposed to be a twin brother of the King of France. He was treated by his attendants with the utmost deference and courtesy. His raiments were of the costliest fabrics. The governor of the citadel in which the "Man in the Iron Mask" was imprisoned, was obsequious in his attentions to the distinguished prisoner. His wishes were observed with the most scrupulous care and the Great Unknown ever ruled his guardians with the sceptre of a king. The prisoner, however, was obliged to wear his iron mask night and day. Any attempt on his part to remove it, meant swift and certain death.

The Ever Watchful Eye.

The feature of his confinement which, perhaps, directly appeals to the world's sympathy, was the human eye that watched his every movement. Through a hole in the door of his apartment, (which was sumptuously furnished,) that eye never relaxed its vigilance. Night and day its ceaseless vigil continued until death's kindly hand relieved the distinguished sufferer from the terror of its unceasing gaze.

And so it was with Cervera and his squadron. The Spanish admiral became the modern "Man in the Iron Mask."

A prisoner behind the lofty hills of San-

**Watched
by
Night and Day.**
tiago, the eyes of Samp-
son's fleet watched the
narrow opening of that
harbor night and day, nor
did their vigilance relax for one second of
time. By night the piercing eye of the electric
search-light closely watched the harbor en-
trance.   The thoughts, the hopes and
prayers of our noble America were all centered upon Sampson and his brave men.
He proved himself to be an excellent fleet
commander and in the twentieth century
his services were appreciated at their just
value.

The glorious victory at Santiago bay, oc-
curring only sixty days after Dewey's target
practice in Manila bay, amazed and electrified the world.   England felt a genuine

**American
Plymouth
Rocks.**
pride in both of these
achievements and point-
ing to America observed:
'' These American roost-
ers are from our own setting and their name
is Plymouth Rock."   When the German
Emperor heard the great news from Santiago very few men in Europe were more
pleased over it.   His joy, however, was
prompted by feelings of self-preservation
rather than from exultation over the American victory.   Wilhelm patted himself on
the back and shook hands with himself for
at least five consecutive hours when he reflected how narrowly he had escaped get-

ting involved in a war with America and
the fortunate escape of his German fleet
from the fate that overtook Cervera's vessels. This is the reason why the German
squadron cleared out of Manila immediately
after Dewey sent his famous request to
Washington to despatch the Oregon to
Manila, "for political reasons." The "bull-
dog of the American navy" reached Manila
in due season but Admiral Von Deiderichs
withdrew long before the "crack of doom"
had ploughed her way into that harbor. As
for France in 1910 she had not yet recov-
ered from her surprise, while to Spain these
disasters proved a paralytic shock of a most
severe character. From 1898 to 1930
Spain was merely walking around to stave
off funeral expenses.

With a relatively strong navy of five hundred and ten (510) war ships to patrol her
coasts in 1999, the United States of the

**Large
Army not
Wanted.**

Americas were not under
any necessity of maintaining a large standing army.
It was fully realized that
an efficient sea-power must be maintained.
With that arm of defence in her possession
the maintenance of a large standing American army can never seriously be entertained.
It has always been a popular belief in
America that if a foreign army of invasion
were to land upon our shores, Americans
would give it a very warm reception, so
spontaneous and effusive in its character

that a majority of the invaders would never
find their way back home again.　Many of
them might become permanent residents in
American soil, so deeply rooted that none
but Gabriel's trump could marshal them
into line again.

Germany in 1899 held the world's medal

**Germany's
Splendid
Army.**

for the finest and best
equipped army, a magni-
ficent engine of war, ready
to move within an hour's
notice, and woe to the enemy that obstructs
its path.　Without any doubt in the closing
period of the nineteenth century the General
staff of the German army was justly regarded as the highest authority in military science.　Such a vast and smooth working
engine for the destruction of human beings
was never before known.　If the sun had
been good enough to stop twelve hours in its
course to accommodate Joshua's beggarly
army, that luminary would no doubt gladly
stand still a whole week on request of the
chief of staff of the German hosts.

In 1899, with a population of barely 50,-
000,000, Germany possessed an army of
2,500,000.　France with much less population had fully as many men under arms.
Russia with a population of over 90,000,-
000 had an army on a peace footing of
3,000,000 men.　The burden upon Europe
was a most crushing one.　In 1899 this
drain was fast sapping the life of those nations, robbing their industries and peaceful

5

avocations of the flower of their youth. This armed state in the time of peace was fully as ruinous as war itself.   No wonder that the Czar of Russia urged a congress of the nations to convene and, if possible, devise some system to reduce these huge armaments.   For this well-meaning attempt to relieve the military burdens of Europe the Russian Czar deserves much credit but, unfortunately, the proposition proved to be impracticable.   The international conference at the Hague in the summer of 1899 secured no definite results.

In 1999 America did not propose to fall into the European snare of maintaining a huge standing army.   When America in 1899 was merely a small Republic, consisting of only forty-five states and a few odd territories, the idea of maintaining a large standing army, on the European plan, was scouted with derision.   In 1899 Americans scoffed at Europe's military establishments as a symbol of Barbarism.   In 1999 when the great American Republic included the entire Western Hemisphere, military rule became more unpopular than ever.   In the twentieth, as in the nineteenth century, America remained firm in her adherence to the Monroe Doctrine.   This wise policy will always prove one of the best safeguards of our American Republic.   Europe must be kept out of the Western Hemisphere.

No Standing Army in 1999.

America will always belong to Americans only. In the twentieth century the Monroe Doctrine lost none of its force, and for many centuries its principles will still remain a living issue.

With a Monroe Doctrine to maintain and defend, it is not surprising to learn that in 1999 the United States of the Americas, with a population of 531,000,000, maintained a small army of 150,000 men. The absolute freedom of America from military burdens in 1899 and 1999 was the glory of the Republic and the envy of a whole world.

The object of government is to guarantee the utmost allowance of freedom to the citizen, and blessed indeed is the nation that can govern itself without having to maintain a huge standing army to hurl at any moment's notice at its neighbors Such barbarism may answer well enough for Europe, whose governments are founded upon wrong principles, but in great, free America, we want none of it, nor never shall.

America always will be the land of the free. Her principles of government are founded upon justice and equity. The voice of the people is heard in the land and it is supreme. The government of the people, by and for the people, is the gift of God to Man and the Almighty has made America the custodian of that priceless jewel.

CHAPTER XIV.

REMOVAL OF THE CAPITAL.

When the Stars and Stripes floated over the Entire
Hemisphere in 1990 Washington, the National
Capital, was removed to Mexico. The name of
the new capital unchanged. Vera Cruz becomes
the Seaport of Washington. The Canal completed in 1915. The new location proves eminently satisfactory to all. The future of China
and the Philippines.

WHEN the good Lord created the earth
He reserved the Western Hemi-
sphere for the exclusive use and control of
the Yankees. They were not slow to avail
themselves of their opportunity. This
comes from force of habit; opportunities
they allow to pass by unimproved are as
scarce as Swiss Admirals. Americans are
warranted to take care of themselves under
any circumstances.

It will surprise no one to learn that in
1999 the Western Hemisphere had passed
in its entirety under the dominion of the
Stars and Stripes. Americans did not
pounce upon and seize the continent, nor
did they even fire one shot to secure its entire control. Canada, Central and South
America simply gravitated towards the
American Union and became absorbed into
one great Republic.

The smaller Republics of the Americas
realized that the United States in 1899 were

a peace-loving nation. Although its army was a mere corporal's guard, America had a population in that year aggregating 75, 000,000. Such a large nation with an insignificant army could mean them no harm. One by one they joined our American Union of their own free will and volition, until in 199, the great American Union became an accomplished fact.

To attempt to rule such a vast stretch of country under any other than the great

It could Govern the World.

Constitution of the United States, would result in a signal failure. The American Constitution, that masterpiece and perfect symbol of human liberty, is great enough and broad enough to govern the entire globe under one flag. Indeed as early as 1999 there were already strong indications that before the expiration of three more centuries such might be the eventual result. It already looked in that year as though the great American Republic would ultimately gather under its wings, Europe, Asia, Africa and the islands of Oceanica.

However, there is a limit to human ambition; there is a boundary to all possibilities. Comparatively speaking, we are dealing

America does not want the Earth.

only with a near future when we behold, in 1999, the proud flag of America, that emblem of liberty which never suffered defeat, floating over

one vast Republic from Alaska to Patagonia.
Other dreamers may hustle for notoriety by
claiming in an aimless way that in 2999
the American flag will float over all the
continents of the world.   They may even
wish to   annex   a few   of   the   planets
under the American flag, but heed them
not.

Daniel Webster's eloquent words: " The
Union, now and forever, one and insepar-
able, " reached a climax when the United
States of the Americas consolidated in
1999.   Nor was there a discordant note in
the grand concert of eighty-five states.
Mason and Dixon's line became a memory
of the past.   The northern states from
Alaska and Canada to Florida ; the middle
states from Mexico to Costa Rica and the
southern states from Colombia to Patagonia,
were all linked together in the bonds of
friendship and brotherly love.   At last
Webster's prophecy had been fulfilled ; the
great Union had become "one and insepar-
able."

To the inquiring mind the question naturally offers itself :   In what manner was the
great American Republic governed in 1999 ?
Were the commands of the Federal government still issued from Washington, D. C.,
or had it been found more convenient to
transfer the seat of government to a locality
better adapted and more central to the new
conditions of the greater Republic ?

In 1990, by decree of Congress of the

UNION
OF THE AMERICAS
IN 1999.

By permission of the Pan-American Exposition Co. of Buffalo, N Y.

United Americas, and at the close of a

Capital transferred to Mexico. special national election held for that purpose, both houses of Congress by a two-thirds vote, elected to transfer the seat of our National government from Washington, D. C., to the city of Mexico, which in 1999, commanded a position midway between the North and South sections of the great Republic. Although transferred by act of Congress to the city of Mexico, our National Capital in 1999 still retained the glorious name of Washington. The name of Washington, D. C., was changed to that of Columbia.

Statesmen in 1990 wisely decided to retain the name of Washington for the National Capital of the great Republic. A few were in favor of retaining the ancient name of Mexico for the new capital but the vast majority of our American voters in 1990 treasured with patriotic love and tenderness the revered name of the Father of his Country. They believed that no matter where the capital of the Republic might be moved to, whether it were located in Brazil or in Alaska, the fame of Washington must go with it and bear the honored association of that name.

Washington, D. C., took the new name of Columbia, having become a city of secondary political importance. The name of Washington belongs to the national capital alone, the home of Congress, the residence of the National Executive and forum of the Supreme Court of the Americas. The hero of Valley Forge and champion of American Independence was still near and dear to every heart in 1990, and may centuries yet unborn honor his memory.

The city of Mexico became the Capital of the Americas for manifold reasons, **Mexico a Natural Centre.** chiefly political, strategical and commercial. To those, who, in 1899 had been accustomed from birth to regard the United States as that narrow strip of country lying between Canada and the Gulf of Mexico, the announcement that the capital of the Americas had been transferred to the city of Mexico, must cause a shock of unpleasant sensation.

It is a human weakness to worship our idols. Woe to those who would destroy them. Tradition must not be tampered with. Americans of 1899 had been taught that a small and beautiful city on the Potomac was the capital of our Federal Union. To them it must come in the nature of a shock to learn that in 1990 the name of that city had changed to Columbia, and Washington, the National Capital, had been transferred to the State of Mexico.

There are, however, other instances on record in which it has been deemed advisable to change the capital of a great nation.

If in the year 1810 an intelligent Russian had announced to his countrymen that the seat of government in Russia would be transferred in 1812 from golden, sacred Moscow to bleak, cold St. Petersburg on the barren swamps of the Neva, his prediction would have been laughed to scorn ; such a statement would have encountered a tempest of derision. Your orthodox Russian would have raved at the mere mention of such an eventuality. In 1810 any intelligent Russian would have regarded the abandonment of ancient Moscow, the custodian of the Kremlin, for a barren spot on the shores of the Baltic, as a positive sacrilege. Yet it is historically true that in 1812 this very thing came to pass.

Instead of uprooting our National Capital from a spot hallowed with sacred tradi-

In Perpetual Sunshine and Flowers. tions and transplanting it into a cold, sterile region, as in the case of the Russian capital, Washington, as a seat of government, was removed from the banks of the Potomac into the splendors of a tropical region,—into the domain of Montezuma and his brave Aztec warriors, where fruits and flowers chase one another in an unbroken circle through the year ; a paradise where the gales are loaded with perfumes of the forests in which birds of radiant plumage and exquisite song fill the air with their delicious melodies.

Washington in 1999 was fast developing into a magnificent city, worthy of its proud

An Earthly Paradise.

name and eminence as the capital of the great American Republic with its population of 531,000,000 people. Built in the heart of the State of Mexico, it was surrounded by magical charms of scenery such as only a tropical paradise may develop. Its lofty domes and spires and stately public buildings, many of them constructed of huge blocks of multicolored glass, were reared amidst a land luxuriant with the cochineal, cocoa, the orange and sugar-cane.

The city of Washington in 1999 was hedged by nature's most subtle art. Beyond the capital's limits were visible a gay confusion of meadows, streams and perpetual flowering forests. From the centre of the new Washington could plainly be seen the majestic outlines of ancient Popocatapetl, rising as a sombre spectre whose rugged head seemed to cleave the skies.

Stretching far away to the right, and clearly visible from the observatory of the Executive Mansion might be seen, towering in its solitary grandeur, the peak of the mighty Orizaba, with its eternal shroud of snow descending far down its sides. How many centuries this mighty giant of the Cordilleras has stood there, a sentinel in the Garden of the Gods, none may tell. But ages and cycles of time after the busy brains of 1899 shall have turned to dust, Orizaba, with the Stars and Stripes adorning its summit, will still rear its proud head and gaze down upon millions of American patriots yet unborn.

The transferment of the capital of the Americas in 1990 to the city of Mexico, was generally regarded as a master-stroke of policy. From a hygienic point of view alone, the change proved eminently a desirable one. Its removal from the malodorous swamps of the Potomac to the elevated plateau upon which the Aztec race reared their ancient capital, with its balmy breezes and tropical luxuriance, proved a most welcome change. It was generally conceded in 1899 that the site of Washington on the malaria-breeding banks of the Potomac, was not a happy selection.

Met with General Approval.

In spite of great precautions several epidemics had devastated the national capital during the decades from 1900 to 1940. Among other pestilential attractions of the Potomac swamps, great prominence was given to a fierce and aggressive tribe of mosquitoes, called "Swamp Angels," which in 1920 increased and multiplied greatly, to the absolute terror of the Washingtonites. It is related of these aggressive and dangerous pests that in 1925 a swarm of them actually carried away a sheep while the animal was grazing upon the White House downs.

But aside from its favorable hygienic considerations the central position of the city of Washington in the State of Mexico commanding the main avenue between North and South America, gave it great political and commercial importance as the capital of the Americas in 1990, one that was enjoyed by no other rival.

The capture and destruction of Washington, in the State of Mexico, could not have **It Became Impregnable.** been effected in 1999 or at any subsequent period. The city in that year became impregnable, so rendered by a vast system or chain of fortresses from the city proper to Vera Cruz, its seaport, a distance of about two hundred miles. The mountain passes and rugged defiles between Washington and Vera Cruz frowned with heavy ordnance. Dynamite guns were ready on every hand to scatter their deadly missles for the edification of all invaders. From Washington to Vera Cruz, great sentinel forts stood in the path of the invader, an unassailable chain, many of them being hardly visible to the eye. Fortifications were constructed upon the high table lands of the Cordilleras, also upon the apex of precipices, and from these dizzy summits shrinking eyes might gaze down two and three thousand feet and admire the bewildering beauties of tropical vegetation. It was estimated by leading engineers in 1999 that with its line of defences to the coast the capital of the United States of the Americas was impervious to the assaults of the world.

The port of Vera Cruz, only two hundred miles east of Washington in a direct line, had been permitted to retain its original name when Mexico became a part and par-

Washington's Outlet to the Sea. cel of the American Union. This concession was made in honor of Cortes, the conqueror of Mexico, the boldest and most intrepid of all warriors of the middle ages, who founded the city of Vera Cruz and destroyed his fleet of vessels so as to compel his followers to wrest from the sway of Montezuma, the city of Mexico. It was at Vera Cruz that Cortes founded the first Spanish colony on the American mainland. In honor and memory of the valiant Spanish commander and his daring exploits in 1520, it was deemed a point of courtesy to retain for that city the baptismal name Cortes had endowed upon it.

In 1999 its spacious harbor was taxed to its utmost capacity to accommodate the world's commerce while en route through the Nicaraguan Canal, which was opened to navigation in 1915, having cost its American investors $195,000,000. The proximity of Vera Cruz to the canal rendered that city an available port, bringing to it a wonderful volume of trade and commerce, and as Vera Cruz in 1999 was merely the ocean outlet of Washington, it will be readily appreciated that the opening of the Nicaraguan Canal and the volume of traffic it diverted in that direction, added materially to the importance of that region as the seat in 1999 of our national government. The completion of the Nicaragua Canal in 1915 was a triumph to the American science of engineering, yet so tardy in conception and execution that it reflected at best only an uncertain honor.   It should have been constructed and opened to navigation as early

Importance of the Canal. as 1885. It was a case of sheer neglect on the part of America. As soon as the Panama bubble exploded and Frenchmen discovered that they had been hoodwinked by speculators, America should have lost no time in constructing the Nicaragua Canal.

The lesson of the Spanish War has taught America the value of an ocean canal connecting the Atlantic and Pacific oceans. With the possession of the Philippines and an enormous Oriental trade the operation of this canal became a factor of the highest importance to America.

An American fleet of warships in the spacious bay of Vera Cruz, only two hundred miles away from Washington, was enabled in 1999 to steam through the canal into the Pacific in only a few hours' time and proceed to Hawaii and the Orient in short order. This was a great improvement on the "good old days" of 1899 when war vessels and transports, leaving New York to go to Manila, had to crawl around the tempestuous Horn or travel via. Suez.

The construction of the interoceanic canal added greatly to the importance of the new location for our National capital in the State of Mexico. Vera Cruz became the rendezvous of the world's commerce. The central location of Washington in the State of Mexico, midway between the two great continents, proved an advantageous and commanding one and was eminently satisfactory to all sections of the great American Republic in 1999.

In considering the vast importance of ocean canal navigation to the Americas, it is well to ascertain what became of the Philippine Islands and China in 1999.

In that year of our Lord, the world was practically governed by three great powers.

Three Great Powers in 1999. The first and greatest of the trio was the vast American Republic, which in that memorable year extended from Alaska to Patagonia. Next came Great Britain, whose sway was undisputed over the vast continents of India, Africa and Australia, along with valuable islands of the seas, like the articles of a traditional auction bill, "are too numerous to mention." The third great Power in

1999 was Russia.   The ruler of all the
Russias was not only Czar of the European
and Siberian domains, but he was also
crowned at the sacred Kremlin as the
Emperor of China.   A glance at the map
of the world will show that in 1999 Russia
was in possession of nearly one-fourth of
the globe's real estate.   Not satisfied with
this, Russian ambition had designs upon
India, intending to employ China as her
base of operations.   England, however,
was always alert and ready to frustrate her
designs.

When the nations of Europe in 1898 were
carving up China, (even Spain and Italy
joining in the scramble for pieces of China-
ware,) Russia, her nearest neighbor on the
north, was careful to secure the biggest
share of the booty.   In 1895 Russia saved
China from the clutches of Japan, for the
philanthropic purpose of doing the stealing
act herself.   After appropriating China's
best provinces on the north, and profiting
by the completion of the Trans-Siberian
railroad in the year 1905, Russian influence
at the court of Pekin, overshadowed all
others.   The Chinese, like all other Orient-
als, believe only what they see.   Russia
had long been their only neighbor in Siberia
but when the great Russian railroad was
completed to Port Arthur, in a very short
period an army of 450,000 well drilled Russian soldiers was bivouacked near the great
wall of China, within rifle shot of Pekin.

Once firmly seated on China's neck, Russian diplomacy moulded the Middle Kingdom as clay in the potter's hand. Its enormous population obeyed implicitly the Czar's ukases, and in 1999 China became a Russian province as completely as the Crimea.

The Russian Emperor of China.

Russia, however, had always entertained a warm friendship and cordial regard for the United States of America ever since the rebellion of 1860-65 and her good wishes were reciprocated on the part of all Americans. Russian respect for America became firmer and more binding as the young American Republic attained its enormous dimensions. Russia, great herself, realized that she had a right to be regarded in the same class as our noble country. As an evidence of Russian esteem for America, during the period from 1920 to 1999, Russia granted to Americans special trade privileges in China in which other nations were not permitted to share.

As a result of these generous concessions to Americans our trade with China in 1999 attained gigantic proportions and nine-tenths of it passed through the Nicaragua canal. So important did our Oriental trade become in the twentieth century that the inter-oceanic canal would have been built even though it had been necessary to pave its channel with bricks of gold and silver. American wheat had largely supplanted rice as the staple food of China, and in 1999 the American export of wheat to China was estimated at a value of $95,000,000. America monopolized nearly the entire Chinese trade in farming implements, electrical machines, cotton goods, dyes and chemicals.

As to the Philippines, the trade with that archipelago was entirely controlled by America. After the proud flag of America had floated one century over those islands, the transformation scene was wonderful. The Filipinos had long learned, after the fall of Aguinaldo, that the American Constitution was broad and big enough to amply protect and to give them that measure of liberty to which all nations are entitled. Long before 1920 they became a docile, patient and laborious people and prospered in an amazing degree. Their exports of hemp, rice and tobacco attained immense proportions and the culture of sugar-cane became so profitable that the Philippines were famed in 1999 as the "Sugar Bowl of the Pacific." America proved a Godsend to those islands. The names of Dewey, Otis and Lawton were held in high esteem for many centuries after Dewey's great victory, which awakened America, electrified the world and gave birth to the grandest Republic the world had ever seen.

Peace and Prosperity Restored.

CHAPTER XV.

ÆRIAL NAVIGATION SOLVED.

Science obtains mastery over the "ethereal blue."
Ærial navigation perfected in 1925. The name
of New York city changed to that of Manhattan.
Washington, in the State of Mexico, becomes
the centre of all airship or ærodrome lines. The
fascinations of ærial navigation. From Manhattan to San Francisco in thirty-six hours, with
stops at Chicago, Omaha and Denver. Terrible
mid-air accidents. An air train cloud bound.

THE Dreamer, thus far, has invited the
attention of the reader to the political
conditions extant in 1999. In the preceding chapters we have contemplated with
feelings exultant, national pride, the superb
growth of the United States of the Americas,
from a comparatively narrow strip of territory in 1899 to a magnificent Republic in
1999, consisting of eighty-five sovereign
States, extending from Alaska to Patagonia,
and embracing in one Republic the continents of North, Central and South America. In order to arrive at a lucid com-
prehension of the political status of the
great American Republic and its relation-
ship towards the world in 1899, we have
reviewed the conditions of other nations of
that period. We must now pass on to the
consideration of other social and economic
conditions which were prevalent in the
American Republic during the twentieth
century.

Do not imagine for one moment that in the brief compass of a century human nature

Human Nature Remains The Same. had changed in any perceptible or appreciable degree. In the year 1899 the traits of humanity were identical with those which were known to the world in the days of the Cæsars. The ebb and flow of human passions, love and hatred in the days of the Pharaohs differed in nowise from those of 1899. If forty centuries did not change our human tendencies, it will not surprise the reader to learn that in 1999 the human family was much the same in its tastes and inclinations as in the nineteenth century.

The eighteenth century was an era of oak and sails ; the nineteenth century proved to be an age of iron, steel and steam, but the twentieth century witnessed far greater strides of improvement resulting from the solution of the ærial navigation problem and the conquest of electricity. The solution of these two great problems alone rendered the twentieth century the most marvelous age of all since the birth of Christ.

Ever since humanity has trodden upon this green, fruitful world of ours ; ever since the gaze of man has turned upward and penetrated the skies, from the days of Adam and perhaps ages before that first settler made his appearance on earth, the problem of ærial navigation has agitated human

breast and brain. To solve this difficult
secret has long been the acme of human
ambition. In 1899 we knew very little
more about ærial navigation than did Noah
and his family in the days when Mt. Arrarat
was first used as a dry-dock.

Quite certain it is that ærial navigation
ten thousand years hence will be limited to

**A
Limited Field
After all.**

a moderate elevation
from the earth. Never
as long as the world en-
dures will human beings
with breath in their nostrils and blood in
their veins reach or travel at an altitude of
over six miles above the earth's surface. We
know this because death would overtake
every venturesome traveler who soared into
those higher regions. A thousand years
hence the laws of nature will still remain
immutably the same.

But the ambition of mankind is to control
the air at a reasonable distance from the
earth's surface and to navigate an element
that is entirely free from all obstructions.
The aim is to so control an ærial machine
that it will not drift before every wind, but
cleave the air and move along its course in
defiance of the storm. To this must be
added a guarantee of safety that the public
is certain to exact before embarking upon
an ærial voyage. Ærial navigation, no
doubt, offers vast attractions but while sailing through the air, with the ease and grace
of a bird, it might prove very inconvenient

for passengers to fall out at a height of a mile or two and land through the roof of some peaceful, happy home or find themselves while unceremoniously falling securely hooked in the fork of a tree.   Such little mishaps in ærial navigation had to be guarded against.

Ærial navigation was perfected about the

The First Airships.

year 1925.   After repeated failures of the Langley system from 1896 to 1920, the learned Washington professor changed his plans.   Instead of endeavoring to lift flat-irons with wings from the ground, and watching turkey buzzards at anchor in the air over the Potomac river, Langley finally created an ærial machine that was operated by electricity and moved by a large, swiftly revolving propeller, somewhat resembling those employed in steam navigation, but with blades at a more abrupt angle.

The flying machines which were constructed from 1920 to 1999 on the Langley plan, were built of Nickalum, an alloy of aluminum, crystalized, within a magnetic field.   The specific gravity of Nickalum, as employed in the manufacture of ærodromes, or flying machines, was .512.   It was lighter than a thin strip of pine wood, malleable as gold and impenetrable as steel.   Ærodromes could not have been successfully manufactured in 1920 if Nickalum had not been employed in their construction.

ÆRIAL NAVIGATION.

This new property was one of the marvelous products of the twentieth century.
It was employed in nearly everything which
required strength and elasticity. It was so
malleable that waterproof garments, over-
coats and shoes were manufactured of Nickalum as early as the year 1912.

With this wonderful and cheaply manufactured metal, ærial navigation became a

**Ærodromes
of
Nickalum.**

possibility. The old
fashion days of silk bal-
loons drifting helplessly
on air currents, had long
passed away. These pre-Adamite curiosities belonged to the period of the nineteenth
century, when man was yet living under
primitive conditions, though by no means
in a state of innocence.

Ærodromes constructed of Nickalum
were largely employed for traveling and
commercial purposes between 1920 and
1925, while in 1999 they had reached a high
stage of perfection. Ærodromes weighing
four hundred pounds only, in 1925, could
easily carry ten persons and cleave their
way like an arrow through a high wind.
Small ærodromes carrying four persons,
weighed only one hundred pounds.

If the wind were favorable on their regular trips, the high grade express ærodrones

**Some
Fast
Traveling.**

in 1999, belonging to the
popular Sky-Scraper line,
could easily make the trip
from Manhattan (former-
ly New York) to Washington, in the State

of Mexico, a distance of 1,949 miles in a direct air-line, in fifteen hours, making brief stops for meals at Columbia, D. C., (formerly called Washington) and at New Orleans. From the Crescent City it was only a short run across the deep, blue gulf, to Vera Cruz, then followed a short spurt of two hundred miles west of Vera Cruz to the national capital, Washington, then built upon the site of the ancient Aztec City of Mexico. In 1999 this was regarded as a neat, breezy little trip.

The name of New York city (always a meaningless and unpopular one), had been **The Great City of Manhattan,** changed in 1912 to the more appropriate one of Manhattan. Its population in 1999 had increased to 25,000,000 souls. Although the largest metropolis of the world, Manhattan in 1999 had reached its zenith.

The consolidation of the republics into one vast American Union, from Alaska to Patagonia, and the removal of Washington as the seat of our national government, from the little District of Columbia to a more central and appropriate location in the State of Mexico, as well as the opening of the Nicaragua Canal, were the leading factors that contributed to the commercial detriment and undoing of Manhattan. The star of destiny shone brightly over Mexico as the conspicuous centre of the new and great American Republic and the volume of

the world's trade passed through the Nicaragua Canal, diverting millions of freight-
age that otherwise must have entered the
port of Manhattan.

The great air-ship or ærodrome building
centre in 1999 was the city of Manhattan.
Upon the Palisades, opposite Grant's tomb
and about one mile east of the lofty Dewey
monument, were stationed vast workshops
for building these beautiful and graceful
ærodromes.   It was ever a fascinating
sight to the men and women of 1999 to see
one of these flying machines starting out of
the shops on its trial trip.   The body of
the ærodrome was resplendent in brilliant
colors and the new airships always appeared in the bravery of bunting and silk flags.

By act of Congress all ærial navigation
companies were obliged to adopt a certain
color and number.   The big express lines
running from Manhattan to Rio ·Janeiro
and Mexico, each adopted a prismatic color
along with their official number.   The object of this was to enable people to distin-
guish at sight an approaching ærodrome
and at once recognize by its color the ærial
line to which it belonged.

The U. S. of the A. ærial express ships
alone were permitted to use white paint on

**Uncle Sam's
Favorite
Color.**

the hull of their æro-
dromes.   Thousands of
them were employed in
the government service
and conveyed troops to all points in the

6

great American Republic. It was, however, strictly forbidden, under severe pen-
alties, to carry any munitions of war or any
explosives or chemicals upon any ærial ship
whatever. The color of black was employed only on funeral occasions. The
ærodrome, which filled the functions of an
ærial hearse in 1999, was painted all black,
hull and sails as well. When the eye could
discern floating in the air and moving
swiftly in one direction a long line of black
ærodromes, it became known that one
more poor mortal had entered into rest,
and his remains were speeding through the
air to their last resting place, namely, the
nearest crematory ; burials of the old style
having been prohibited by act of Congress
in 1947 throughout the United States of
the Americas.

It was a really thrilling sight to see the
large ærodromes in their brilliant colors
sailing through the air with such swiftness
and graceful ease, each one carrying over
its stern the flag of the great Republic with
its eighty-five stars. Like beautiful phan-
toms they flitted by, gracefully, noiselessly,
swiftly cleaving the air without the least
apparent effort. It was an inspiring sight.

Bridal couples in 1999 were frequently
married in an ærodrome as it rested on a

**Airship
Wedding
in 1999.**

city square or in a modest
village green. Standing
around the airship, which
was always decorated
with multi-colored flags and floral designs,

were invited guests, friends and spectators. After the ceremony was over and congratulations exchanged, the minister, as well as the nearest relatives alighted from the ærodrome, which immediately commenced to ascend amidst the hand-clappings, hurrahs and Godspeeds of the gathering. As the ærodrome gracefully arose about ten feet above terra firma, a few handsful of rice were thrown at the happy pair, who retaliated by throwing roses and other flowers at their friends below. When the ærodrome attained a height of about one hundred feet, the navigator steered the ærial ship in the direction required and the journey then commenced.

The trip across the continent in an ærial ship was always, in pleasant weather, a delightful experience. A voyage from Manhattan (formerly New York), to San Francisco, was a matter of about thirty-six hours, with stops at Chicago, Omaha and Denver. Sailing through balmy summer skies, with a continent at one's feet, was an experience never to be forgotten. It was exhilarating to glide unchecked, without noise or friction, dust or smoke, over lakes, valleys, plains and mountains. All sense of danger or fear was banished from the mind.

At night the ærodromes were compelled by law to travel at half speed, with two searchlights, fore and aft, in constant operation. The port lights of all ærodromes were red, and the starboard lights were green. These precautions were rendered necessary in order to avoid mid-air collisions. Some disasters in 1999 filled the

Ærodrome Collisions in Mid-air.
country with alarm. In 1940 a terrible mid-air collision occurred over Rio Janeiro. Two swift ærodromes, attached to the Mercury Limited express, collided about 2,000 feet over that city causing a serious loss of life. Collision in mid-air was always the nightmare and dread of ærial navigation. People in 1999 had not yet become fully reconciled to the delightful sensation of dropping out of the clouds and getting their clothes torn on church steeples and lightning rods. When they made a start for heaven they were better prepared to make it from earth as a starting point, rather than making a break for paradise starting from the clouds.

Accidents, unfortunately, were of frequent occurrence. In the columns of the *Hourly Journal*, published in the city of Manhattan, (old New York,) under date of Thursday, July 17, 1984, we find the following harrowing narrative :

MID-AIR COLLISION !

The Comet Express Collides with the Milky Way
Ærostatic Express.

Twenty-five Passengers Dashed to Earth.

Many Saved in the Descent by Using the Air-Life
Preservers.

Manhattan, N.Y., 2 p. m., July 17, 1984.—A mid-air collision resulting in the death of twenty-five persons, and injuries to many others, occurred at 11 o'olock this morning at a distance of 2,500 feet over the city of Binghamton, N. Y.

The Transcontinental Comet Express, San Francisco to the eastern coast, which passes Denver at 10 p. m., takes its easterly flight and passes over Binghamton about 11 o'clock on the following day. The west bound Milky Way Express is due over Binghamton at about the same hour.

A heavy fog arising from the Susquehanna prevailed at the time and this, added to the fact that a propeller-blade of the Comet Express was disabled, caused the collision, which collapsed the ærodrome of the Milky Way, capsizing twenty-five of the passengers, many of whom fell in the Court House green, being buried in the sod under the terrific velocity of the fall. One passenger from Cobleskill, who had just started for a trip to the Yellowstone Park, fell on the statue of Justice on the dome of the Court House. At noon his legs had not yet been extricated. The city is plunged in gloom. Among the killed were five passengers from Sidney, Unadilla and Bainbridge. The details of their death are too shocking for recital. The bodies were taken to the Binghamton crematory and burned. The ashes will be forwarded to-morrow to the relatives.

On the Comet Express from San Francisco, the passengers were more fortunate. The navigator calmed the fears of the passengers, many of whom were ready to jump overboard and take a short cut into Binghamton, frenzied as they were through fear. Those who jumped were careful to adjust the air life preserverers before leaping. The Comet Express passengers landed in Binghamton safely.

Gen. Burgess had both legs so badly broken that they will have to be amputated. The surgeons will supply new electrical limbs that will prove fully as serviceable as the natural ones.

Terrible accidents like the one above described, taken from the columns of the *Hourly Journal*, under date of July 17, 1984, were not by any means the only class of accidents caused in the twentieth century by ærial navigation. Under the influences of sighing breezes, an invigorating atmosphere and a mild, genial sun, nothing could be more delightful than a mid-air excursion on board of an ærodrome. Nothing could exceed the pleasant sensations one experiences while noiselessly gliding over tree-tops and church spires.

In 1999 courtships were no longer conducted in the locality of the much abused garden gate. Love's trysting-place was often transferred to the roof of the paternal house, where the coy damsel frequently awaited with anxious heart for the arrival of her lover on an airship.

But, with all its bright attractions, ærial navigation had dangers of its own, obstacles and difficulties. Here we have another illustration of the perils of ærial navigation. We copy the following article from the columns of the Sidney *Record*, under date of Jan. 15, 1999, which goes to prove that ærodromes, like all mortals here below, had troubles of their own :

CLOUD-BOUND.

THE UTICA ÆROSTATIC TRAIN DELAYED BY A MID-AIR STORM.

SIDNEY, N. Y., Jan. 15.—There is a cloud-blockade on the line of the Oregon & New York Ærostatic Transit Co., and the air train which left Vancouver last evening is stalled at a point 3,000 feet above Norwich, with little prospects of getting away for several hours.

Cloud-plows have been sent up from Syracuse, but so dense is the raging ærial snow that the plows have been unable to reach the stranded train. The storm is the most severe one known in years in this locality and came on at 8 o'clock last night. It raged over the city of Sidney all night, although no snow fell.

The Weather Bureau in Washington, Mexico, pronounces it one of the familiar mid-air storms and places its lowest point at 3,000 feet above Sidney and its highest at 5,000, making a storm stratum of 2,000 feet. The clouds are banked for a distance of thirty miles and are almost impenetrable.

The conditions are such as to make telepathic messages to the conductor of the air train difficult to deliver. A message, however, was received saying that all are well on board and the etherize heating apparatus working well.

In the same edition of that paper, on the first page, was published another account of a serious accident, in which an air-ship soared too high and broke away from the attraction of the earth's gravity. It read as follows:

AIR SHIP MISSING.

THE PONTIAC TEN DAYS OVERDUE AT VERA CRUZ.

WASHINGTON, Mexico, Jan. 14, 1999.—The Transoceanic air-freighter Pontiac has been overdue at

Vera Cruz for ten days. It is feared the ship has got snarled in the upper ether currents. As she has not been spoken by other air-ships it is probable she has drifted away from the influence of the earth's gravitation, and drawn into the orbit of some neighboring planet. It may land in Mars.

Ærial navigation in 1999 was not merely confined to large express, passenger and freight ships, but also came into general use by the public. The Ærocycle of the twentieth

Everybody in the Air.

century was an ærial bicycle that skimmed through the air with admirable ease, being operated like the old-fashioned bicycles suffering mortals in 1899 used to jump over hills and rough roads, straining muscle and nerve to the utmost tension, and frightening horses with their "bicycle face." Two or three of the bicycles of 1899 were kept as curiosities in a glass case in 1999 in the war department at Washington, Mexico. They were regarded as instruments of voluntary torture, relics of a species of refined barbarism. The invention of the Ærocycle sealed the doom of bicycles.

CHAPTER XVI.

THE AGE OF ELECTRICITY.

Ærial navigation shunned by many people in 1999. The great Age of Electricity. The Passing of the Horse. The noble beast loses its fetters and becomes a Household Pet. Steam engines a relic of the past. No more smoke in railroad travel. Tunnels lighted bright as day and filled with pure air. Single-rail electric roads all the go.

IT must not, however, be imagined that people in 1999 passed away their whole lives traveling in the air. Millions could not be induced under any consideration, to plant a foot in any ærial ship. They hugged old Mother Earth with a true devotion worthy of a better cause. Many people in the year 1899 were to be found who entertained strong antipathies against traveling on water, but in 1999 the opponents **Old Earth** of ærial navigation outnumbered them one hundred **Good Enough** dred to one. For this **for Them.** and other more important reasons, the genius of the twentieth century applied itself assiduously to the perfecting of electrical and compressed air machines of every conceivable character.

The twentieth century saw the coup-degrâce, or death blow, given to sails for propelling ships, horses used for traction purposes and steam in mechanical engineering.

Electricity, drawn directly from coal, as well as the air, was procurable in inexhaustible quantities. Electricity long before 1999 was stored with the utmost ease and economy, and shipped all over the world for lighting, heating and motive power. The partnership existing between the old-fashion steam engine and electric dynamos was dissolved forever in 1920. Electricity conducted the business alone and in its own name after steam and its clumsy accessories withdrew from the firm.

One of the first to feel the effects of the change was that greatly **Good-bye** admired and beloved crea-**Mr. Horse.** ture, the horse. In 1999 plenty of horses were yet to be found in the haunts of civilization. They were generally kept as pets, gentle, graceful and docile creatures, reminders of past centuries in which their progenitors had so laboriously served the ends of man. Occasionally in 1999 some old-fashioned swell, who had been acquainted with horses and their ways in 1930, would occasionally harness up a pair to a curious looking vehicle with shafts and take a short drive, but in 1999 such antiquities were regarded with the same curiosity Noah might have experienced could he have seen an ærodrome circling around the ark. Out in the country, in remote districts and mountain regions, horses were occasionally seen doing farm work, but the sight was an unusual one, invariably attracting much attention. It was estimated in 1999 that in about one hundred more years the horse in cities and country towns would become as rare as the buffalo.

In 1930 when the horse had already ceased to be a beast of burden, epicures openly accepted its flesh as a highly esteemed dish. Indeed it became quite the fad for fast swells to dine on trotter steak. The dray and carriage horses were the first ones to disappear, but the racers held on pretty well. In 1942 the turf and paddock were still popular, though rapidly declining.

The competitors that drove the horse from its field of labor were the electric and compressed air horseless vehicles. As early as 1899 the horseless carriage was rapidly striding into popularity. In 1920 they were common sights everywhere. In 1950 they had crowded the horse to the wall and in 1999 horseless vehicles for business or pleasure were exclusively employed everywhere.

Horses in 1999 were no longer beasts of burden in the great American Republic.

Emancipated by Electricity. They had been emancipated by electricity and compressed air. In remote sections of the American Republic, like the pampas of the State of Brazil and the mountain regions of the State of Peru, horses were frequently to be seen, but seldom employed as beasts of burden. It took many centuries to wipe the equine race from the face of the globe.   The history and achievements of the noble brute had been for many centuries linked to that of man. In 1999 the Arab still loved his faithful charger, guarding it as the apple of his eye.   The noble animal still shared his tent.   In his estimation a wife or two were of little worth compared with the swift, graceful animal that so often carried him from danger and left his pursuers in the rear.   It would have been sad indeed for the world, so early as 1999 to lose an animal endowed by nature with so much intelligence, an animal that again and again had decided a thousand fields of battle and had braved all dangers by land or sea.   But from the thraldom of labor, the horse in 1999 had been emancipated and this tribute was one worthy of his peerless fame.

Even the reindeer of the Polar regions felt the touch of twentieth century genius. The Laplander had no further use for the dog-power of his ancestors.   His sleds glided along the fields of ice, propelled by electricity, of which inexhaustible supplies were drawn from the aurora borealis.

In 1999 automobiles required only three days to traverse the distance from Montreal in the American State of East Canada to Washington, our national capital in the State of Mexico. The roads throughout the Americas had reached a high grade of perfection and travel on electric automobiles

Good Roads Everywhere. became a pleasure even in all the Southern States of the American Union, such as Venezuela, Bolivia, Colombia, Ecuador, and Argentine. Uncle Sam's farm in 1999 was a big one and was covered with good roads. Horses and steam engines were altogether too slow for the twentieth century.

The exclusion of steam from all railroads in 1999 proved a great boon to travel. Railroad smoke was a drawback to steam roads, while sparks, cinders and live coal were a constant danger to property. When a happy bride and groom took their departure on a train for their honeymoon in 1899 their friends pelted them with rice, while the old fashion steam engine attached to the train rounded the compliment by pelting the newly wedded pair with cinders and soot. Dense volumes of black smoke

Delights of Steam Travel. poured into the railway coaches, filling everycrevice and corner, rendering the human face unrecognizable. Travelers in these old-fashioned cars, clad in the bravery of fashion, in their silks and fine raiment, would journey only a short distance when they would become almost unrecognizable from the torrents of black soft-coal smoke that pierced their cuticle and darkened their lives. It was hard to determine at the end of a brief journey of a thousand miles whether the white man who bought a through ticket in New York was a Caucasian or an Ethiopian when he landed in Chicago, so dense was the smoke through which he had traveled.

The delightful atmosphere of a tunnel formed one of the great attractions of steam travel in the good old days of 1899. Our unhappy American travelers while journeying on these steam roads would suddenly be rushed into a black hole, the damp and foul air of which was enough to kill a salamander, filled with smoke and asphyxiating gases. The marvel is that one-half of the people ever pulled through a tunnel alive.

In 1999 these monstrosities of steam railroad travel were entirely done away with. Not a steam engine was anywhere to be found. The single rail electric railroad was monarch of all it surveyed, and there were none to dispute its sway. It ruled the universe. The new-born electrical power drew its forces from the air. Electricity was greater than light itself. Its rule was felt by day as well as by night.

The Single Rail is King.

In 1999 when an electric train dashed through a tunnel, its arch was aglow with electric fire, rendering the passage light as at noon time in a blazing sun. A touch of the button turned on every light in the coaches. The air of the tunnel, instead of being black with smoke and noxious vapors, was pure as the open air. Travel was rendered delightful in these swift-speeding trains on the single-rail electric railroads, which easily maintained a speed of two miles per minute. In point of speed they were easily outwinged by the ærodromes, but for all that, grass did not have much time to grow under the gearing of any electric car in 1999.

These single-track electric railroads covered the Americas like a network of cobwebs. They were much safer than the two-track system of railroads peculiar to the old period of 1899, when steam engines, going around curves at two miles per minute, were liable to lose their heads and lay down in the ditch to try and figure out where they were at. The single rail upon which the electric car was balanced in 1999, was built about three feet above the track. The cars were so constructed that the wheels ran along their whole length, the sides of the car being built to a point about two feet below the rail. The trolley wire overhead gave more steadiness to the car. It could not upset.

Two Miles per Minute.

Through lines from Chicago to Washington, in the State of Mexico, attained high speed, as well as the electric lines that crossed the isthmus from the State of Mexico to Rio Janeiro. It frequently hap-

pened that strawberries gathered at the base
of Mt. Orizaba, in Mexico, were delivered
in Chicago in season for supper the
same day.   Fish of highly esteemed flavor
that were swimming in the bay of Vera Cruz
at break of day were frequently placed on ice
and reached Manhattan in time for dinner at
seven p. m. the same day.

CHAPTER XVII.

ELECTRICAL NAVIGATION.

Strange and novel uses to which electricity was applied in 1999. Hydrophobia banished from the earth. The relations of Creditor and Debtor greatly improved. Electrical ocean, river and lake navigation. The ocean ablaze with electric lights. Ships navigated by wireless telegraphy.

IT has always been the conceit of every age that its own era is the most progressive and the most enlightened of all. In 1799 any man who could have stood on the deck of Nelson's flagship "Victory" and informed that gallant sailor that in 1899 warships would navigate without sails; that powder would be used that made no smoke; that heavy rifles would hurl a ton shell fourteen miles, would have been dropped overboard as a monumental liar.

The age in which we live is always a conceited one; always ready to scoff at innovations. Every age had a bump of its own. How these precious bumps are smoothed down one by by one, is really interesting. The stage coach was king in its day. As men gazed upon the lumbering, six miles per hour coach, the bump of the period˙made them believe it was the swiftest and most luxurious mode of travel the world would ever see. Steam came and reduced the stage

The Bump of The Age.

coach bump.   When men saw steam loco-
motives drawing fast trains and covering
the country with villainous smoke, they
really believed it was the swiftest mode of
travel the world ever would employ.   Electricity then appeared and reduced the steam
bump.

In 1999 electricity became a mighty monarch and an obedient slave.   It ruled and
it obeyed.   This lively
king of the twentieth
century was a hustler.
Sixteen   distinct   trips
around the globe it could make in just one
second's time.   Electric railroads and flying
machines could not reasonably hope to
make sixteen separate trips around the
globe in one second's time.   The age of
1999 was a very rapid one, but its joints
were too rheumatic to attempt any such
gait.   A traveler hustling around the world
at the rate of sixteen times per second
would hardly have time to visit and shake
hands with friends.

A Lively Customer.

In the twentieth century electricity,
the servant-king of the world, was har-
nessed to everything con-
ceivable. Everything was
done by merely pressing
a button.   Houses built
in that period had no stairs.   Every private house had its elevator.   Press a button and up it went.   Houses built in that
period had no chimneys.   All heating and

All Done by Electricity.

every bit of the cooking was done by electricity. If you wanted heat, press a button ; more heat wanted, press two. Locks and keys also became relics of a past age. No one in 1999 ever locked his house. Every house was provided with an electrical outfit. Those who desired to leave the house for a few hours attached the electric gongs and alarm bells. When connection was made no one could leave or enter the house without raising a pandemonium and sending an alarm to the central police station.

The uses of electricity in 1999 were carried to even absurd lengths. Man's most faithful, but, alas, uncertain friend, the dog, was in evidence throughout the twentieth century. He wagged his tail vigorously as ever in token of kindnesses received. He was as ready as ever to sacrifice his life for that of his master, as well as to plant his teeth into the calf of his leg. The Hindoo charmer is never really safe until he has extracted the fangs of the reptile.

And so it was with the twentieth century dog. Nothing can be more violent than death by hydrophobia. The bite of the dog may prove more terrible than that of the cobra. This scourge was effectually removed. In 1999 dogs over one year old had their teeth removed by electricity. Their mouths were then fitted with a false set. During dog-days, while Sirius was in the ascendant, the false teeth were removed and all canines were kept on a vegetable diet.   Hydrophobia became one of the lost arts.

Another peculiar method in which electricity was utilized in 1999 tended to rob dentistry of some of its terrors.   There was one feature of dentistry in 1899 that often tested the best nerves, and that was the peculiar odor common to all dental chambers of horror.   This peculiar odor settles like a cloud upon the stomach and seldom appeals in vain to one's nerves for sympathy.   For this reason an electrical machine was invented in 1999 which enabled the patient to remain at home while an offending tooth was tendering its resignation.   The dentist, during the operation, remained in his den, enjoying a monopoly of its odors.   If a tooth ached all one had to do was to call up a dentist, on the telephone, and ask to be placed on the line.   The victim, in the seclusion of his back parlor, adjusted the electrical forceps and signalled to the dentist, five blocks away, to touch it off, then the festivities commenced.   These private tooth extracting séances became very popular.   No profane eyes were there to witness the agony of the victim, as in a public dental office.   If he shouted loud enough to make a hole in the sky or tried to kick the plaster off the ceiling, no one was any

Electrical

Dentistry.

the wiser for it. But in a public dental office (especially with ladies in the adjoining
room), while the victim is being harpooned,
his eloquent groans must be stifled and no
attempt must be made by the victim to kick
at the chandeliers. The new system of
home electrical tooth extracting proved very
popular. It was one of the things that had
come to stay.

In 1999, through the medium of electricity, the relations existing between creditors
and debtors became closer and more bind-

Sure Cure for Dead Beats. ing. In 1899, for some
reason or other never
fully explained, a debtor
who had a long standing
account, was liable to dodge into some nook,
corner or side street, if he caught a glimpse
of his creditor coming down the road. The
relations existing between creditor and
debtor in the nineteenth century were not
as cordial as they should be. If the debt
were of long standing there lacked a certain
warmth in their greeting which was perhaps
difficult to account for.

In 1930 creditors and debtors adjusted
themselves in better harmony, at least they
kept in closer electrical touch with one
another. If the sum due was $50 or over
and of long standing, the law allowed the
creditor to connect his debtor with an electrical battery. The object of this wise law
was to keep the creditor in constant touch
with his debtor. If the debt was over three

months due, the creditor was allowed to occasionally "touch up" his debtor without having to hunt him up and dun him. The creditor always had him "on the string" so to speak. It was further specified by law that creditors must employ only as many volts as there were dollars due on account in shocking a debtor. These electrical shocks were merely reminders, intended to refresh the memory of the debtor. A man owing $200 was liable to receive two hundred volts until the debt was satisfied.

This plan for the collection of bad debts worked very successfully. In 1999 no

Worked Like a Charm.

debtor could tell when his creditor might touch him up. The shock reminding him of his old debt might come during the night and disturb his pleasant dreams. Perhaps while seated at the family table, or perhaps even while engaged in family worship, an electric shock might come that would raise him three feet off the floor. Such little occurrences were rather embarrassing, especially if the debtor was talking at the time to some lady friend. A man owing $500 was in danger of his life. His creditor was liable to dun him by giving him a shock of five hundred volts. Such sensations, certainly, are not as pleasant as watching a yacht race, with your boat an easy winner.

A curious illustration of the operation of this new condition between creditors and bad debtors, by which the former had an electrical control of the latter, came to light in a parish church on the banks of the St. Lawrence. It appears that the village school teacher, who was also choir-master, was busy with a Saturday evening rehearsal. The members of the choir were in their places, while the professor stood near the communion-rail, facing the choir, with his back turned towards the empty pews. He was speaking, when suddenly his red hair stood on end, his whiskers straightened out at right angles, while his eyes looked big as door knobs. He then gave a leap in the air, turned a somersault backwards and cleared ten pews before landing again on his feet. It appears that he owed his land-lord an old board bill of $120 and the latter had just given him an electrical dun. The choir was astounded at the professor's per-formance. The latter excused himself and merely said it was a slight attack of grip.

In 1942 any one who used the word "steamship" was immediately rated a back number. A few of them, it is true, still fouled the ocean with their villainous smoke, but in 1999 the electrical ship ploughed the briny waters. It was a grand sight to see a magnificent ship nine hundred feet in length propelled through the waters at a

Electrical Ocean Navigation. rate of thirty-five knots per hour by an invisible power, a mighty giant encased in the interior of the ship, a power that labored silently yet swiftly, with no perceptible vibration to the vessel and without emitting volumes of black smoke.   These swiftly moving electrical ships were strange and striking in their appearance.   Those constructed in 1975 by the Cramps had no masts, and they, of course, had no more use for funnels than a hen has for teeth.   To the people of the old school of 1899, the ocean electrical ship looked strange indeed.   The spectacle of a large steamship of 28,000 tons burden cleaving the ocean waves at the rate of forty knots per hour, with no masts and no smokestacks, looked strangely to men in 1975 who had been accustomed in their youth to old fashioned steamships like the City of New York, Campagnia, Kaiser Wilhelm der Gros, Fürst Bismarck, Teutonic and others of that class.   In 1975 the hull of the electrical ship retained practically the same old lines.   An electrical ship, like the Great Republic, built in the year last named, plying between Manhattan and Liverpool, was a trifle over nine hundred feet long, with only eight-two feet breadth of beam.   From stem to stern was built a swell body roof which covered the entire deck of the vessel.   This covering was supported by ornamental iron columns from the bulwarks and usually stood about twenty feet above the deck.   The only object that arose above the deck-roof was the captain's bridge, in which was stationed the steersman, who steered the leviathan by

merely pressing electrical buttons on a
small disc in front of him. With the masts
and funnels removed from an electrical
ocean ship, much valuable room was thus
secured, adding greatly to the comfort of
the passengers.

Electricity was pressed into every conceivable service. That wonderful element
was man's best and most
**Lighting Up
the
Atlantic.**
faithful servant. There
was no duty in the twen-
tieth century too menial
for it to do. It transformed our ocean,
lake and river craft into a blaze of light by
night. Collisions after dark were unknown
to navigation in 1975. At a distance of ten
miles out at sea an electrical vessel looked
like a solid mass of moving flame. Electricity drawn directly from the air and extracted from coal, costs practically nothing.
The chief item of expenditure was to maintain the electrical machines in repair. In
1899 sailing ships moved along at a snail
gait and during night time a small green
and red lamp on the port and starboard
sides of the ship was all that enabled other
vessels to note their presence. It was always the marvel of that age that a hundred
collisions did not take place every night on
the Atlantic. But in 1999 not a sail or
steamship was anywhere to be seen, on
ocean, lake or river. Electricity was
cheaper, swifter and more reliable.

In 1899 so backward was the age that

7

small boats, called row-boats, were still propelled with oars. In that year those primitive people still employed the old methods of propelling a boat that were in vogue in the days of the Phoenicians and Vikings. They still rowed a boat in the manner of the Greek galley slaves. In 1930 seamen had no more use for oars than a sperm whale has for paddle-wheels. Everything that could float, from a wash-tub to a man-of-war, was propelled by electricity. Even toy boats, sold for $5, were propelled by electricity. The winds still raged in 1999. From zephyr to cyclone that element ruled over the surface of the globe, but man had little use for it. Even the staid Hollander harnessed the wind no more. His mills were run by electricity, while the same agency was continually at work pumping out his dykes.

Through the agency of electricity navigation in the twentieth century was rendered much safer. The ocean by night was dotted with electric buoys, which tossed and bowed with every wave. On these buoys signal-lights were placed, and passing vessels could read the latitude and longitude in which they were in at any time of the day. The figures were plainly marked on each buoy. By night the Atlantic ocean between Sandy Hook and Daunt's Rock was dotted with bright electric arc lights of 8,000 c. p. The eye never wearied gazing upon the picturesque beauty of the scene.

The effect of these brilliant lights on the broad bosom of the ocean, especially during **A Scene of Thrilling Beauty.** a storm, was grand beyond the power of pen to describe. A distant wave could be clearly seen approaching one of these electric, mid-ocean buoys. On it sweeps, a tremendous current that no human power could stem. The rugged blue wall of the great wave glistens in the dazzling electric light as its huge side and foaming crest reaches the electric buoy. It seems as though the light and buoy must be swept to destruction and buried from sight. As the great wave sweeps over the light, all becomes dark for a few seconds, but when the mighty billow has swept on, the electric arc again blazes forth in the trough of the sea bidding defiance to Neptune's frowns. These mighty mid-ocean scenes, viewed from the deck of an electric ocean greyhound, were thrilling in the extreme.

Along the great chain of coast-line of the United States of the Americas, from the State of Maine to the States of Venezuela, Brazil and Patagonia, also on the Pacific slope from the States of Chile, Peru and Colombia to the States of West Canada and Alaska, every rock or promontory dangerous to navigation, was ablaze with electric beacons. Electricity was common as air. Oceans and continents were made more habitable to man. It became in 1999 the world's sun by night.

The perfect and absolute control of electricity by the scientists of the twentieth century benefited both aerial and ocean navigation, in furnishing the motive power. But these were benefited in another and hardly less remarkable manner by the perfected Marconi system of wireless telegraphy, which in the nineteenth century was comparatively unknown and in its early experimental stage. In aerial and ocean navigation wireless telegraphy proved an invaluable aid. The bright, young Italian inventor became a benefactor of the human race.

CHAPTER XVIII.

WIRELESS TELEGRAPHY.

The great advantages of wireless telegraphy in navigation. Ships are enabled to communicate with shore during voyages. Messages received and sent at any time en route. Collisions at sea reported at once. Belated steamers cause no anxiety.

IN the old-fashioned days of sails and steam, when a vessel left port and passed out of sight, she instantly became a whole world in herself. Communication nad been severed with the outer world. The condition of a sailing vessel during a calm was a picture of helplessness. Steamships were more self-reliant—they at least controlled their own course. But both classes of ships, whether propelled by sail or steam, once out of sight of land, were temporarily shut out from the busy world.

During these enforced absences upon an ocean voyage, great events frequently happened of which passengers, officers and crews were necessarily ignorant of. At the **Shut Out of the World.** termination of a long or short voyage, the first news could only be obtained from the pilot-boat which met the approaching vessel far out at sea. War might be on the eve of declaration as the vessel left port, battles might be fought, the enemy might be vanquished and even peace declared and a knowledge of all these events would only reach the tardy mariner upon the arrival of the vessel at her port of destination.

Such a condition of affairs, often the cause of the deepest anxieties on the part of ocean travelers, might answer well enough for the days of the Crusaders, when kings of Great Britain went to Palestine to battle for the Cross, and never again heard from home in three or four years' time. When Napoleon, that meteor of the nineteenth century, left the shores of *la belle France* for the rocky desolation of St. Helena, it was over a year before he received any news from Paris. The same conditions ruled in 1899. Steam had rendered ocean voyages shorter and more punctual. But the main difficulty still existed. Passengers on our ocean-liners during a voyage knew as little of occurrences at home as those who traveled in the days of the Vikings and Crusaders. In this respect (as in many others), the world in 1899 was no better off than in the days when the Roman legions landed on the shores of Britain. The nineteenth century and the centuries before Christ were upon equal footing in this respect.

Many splendidly equipped steamships, with colors flying and bands playing left port in the old days of sails and steam, with multitudes waving their adieux and heartily wishing them God-speed and were never again heard from. No communication was possible in those days between land

and vessels at sea. Sometimes they were

**Into the
Jaws
of Death.**

doomed in the cold embrace of an iceberg; an occasional collision sent hundreds of souls to their final account; fire, always dreaded on the ocean, caused many to suffer the horrors of thirst and starvation; the ocean claimed its victims in many dreadful forms and no tidings ever reached home of the fate of loved ones, because communication between ship and shore in the "good old days" of 1899, was impossible. This supreme difficulty had not yet been overcome in 1899, and the defect was universally regarded as being a most deplorable one. The only communication ever maintained between vessels in mid-ocean and the main shore in the nineteenth century was done by cable-ships, while actually engaged in laying an ocean cable. The Great Eastern was the first steamship to lay claim to this distinction, when in 1867, her officers fished up and brought to the surface the broken Atlantic cable and the great news was flashed from ship to shore.

Vessels in those days of the nineteenth century only too often left port never again

**A Very
Backward
Age.**

to be seen by mortal man. Loved ones plunged into a watery grave, locked in each other's embrace, and none survived to tell the fearful tale. Communication with shore was unknown in the vaunted civilization of the nineteenth century. The fate of the Naronic, of the White Star line, looms up in evidence. Not a whisper was again heard of her after she left port. The City of Glascow in 1854 sank in Neptune's pastures. Four hundred and eighty souls went down in that brave ship. No hint, however slight, was ever heard of her. The Ocean Monarch, the Pacific of the Collins line, and the ill-fated City of Boston, all suffered fates that none but the day of judgment can reveal.

This confession of weakness, this serious drawback of the nineteenth century, which added to the terrors of those "who go down into the great deep," was fortunately not shared by the advanced sciences and arts of the twentieth century. Wireless telegraphy contributed almost as much to the comfort of ocean and ærial navigation as electricity. Telegraph poles that rendered hideous some of our most beautiful avenues and the antiquated ocean cables were entirely relegated into oblivion. The former went into the scrap heap, while the latter found their way into Davy Jones' locker.

Long before 1999 wireless telegraphy was employed on all vessels on ocean, river and lake. Instant communication was at all times maintained between ship and shore.

It Opened a New Era. War vessels at foreign stations made their daily reports in 1999 to the Navy Department in the State of Mexico. All other navies of the world enjoyed the same facilities. Relatives telegraphed to their families and friends from vessels in mid-ocean. It was quite common to receive a brief message from an Atlantic liner two thousand miles east of Sandy Hook, as follows :

On board Electrical Ship Manhattan. }
Latitude 50 N., long. 30 W. }

Dear Henry :—Got over being seasick. Baby and nurse doing nicely. Had strawberries and cream for dinner. Dodged an iceberg and struck a whale, yesterday. Love to all. Will wireless from Paris.

ETHEL.

Overdue vessels in 1999 gave no anxiety in that era of progress. If a shaft broke the home office was at once notified that the vessel would be several days behind her schedule time in arriving at her destination. If caught in a fog or obliged to move at half speed, the information was immediately lodged on shore. In fact it even became possible to navigate vessels from the shore.

In 1982 the strange experiment was made of navigating a large ocean electric ship

Sailed his Ship from Land. from Manhattan (old N. Y.), to Queenstown. The name of the vessel was the City of Sidney.

After the pilot had dropped off at the Hook, Captain Sherman, of the Electric Belt Line of vessels, remained in his private office in the forty-third story of Anti-Trust building on 59th street, Manhattan, and issued his commands by wireless telegraph to the first officer of the City of Sidney. Reports

reached the captain every six hours, giving
the exact latitude and longitude and the
ship's course was directed from the captain's
private office on 59th street in the city of
Manhattan.   In other words it was the city
of Manhattan that kept the City of Sidney
on the move, so to speak.   The ship's
course, conduct of the crew, the health of
the passengers, the reports of passing electrical vessels, the velocity of wind and other
details of navigation, were communicated
to Captain Sherman, whose orders were
given and obeyed as readily as though issued
from the bridge or deck of the City of Sidney.   When that vessel arrived off Queenstown to land the U. S. of the A. mails,
Capt. Sherman in 59th street ordered half
speed and finally stopped the electric engines.   Of course, while navigating his immense vessel across the ocean and remaining seated in his office at home, Captain
Sherman could not assume his place in the
saloon at the head of the table.   Wireless
telegraphy could not, with all its ingenuity,
satisfy one's appetite at the sumptuous dinners served on board the City of Sidney.
But this demonstrated to the world
in 1982 that with wireless telegraphy com-
manders could remain in their office on
shore and sail their ships to foreign ports in
perfect safety.   This was done in 1982 just
as easily as the old style train despatcher
controled far away trains in 1899 while
seated in his own office.

The Marconi system of wireless telegraphy, when perfected in 1920, employed
the Hertzian magnetic waves, which are
identical with the waves of light. Whenever an electric spark is made to leap from
one electrode to another, one of these waves
is created. The Marconi instruments for
sending and receiving are tuned to each
other and are then invulnerable to the attack of waves of different lengths.

These rays of electricity are reflected and
directed in a given direction like rays of
light. An electric circuit
A Marvelous with a key, gives the
Invention. basis of the Marconi system. This circuit runs
through a spark coil with an oscillator to
produce continuous electric sparking so long
as the circuit is kept closed by the key—and
from this the sparking wires run out of
doors to the pole from which the messages
are sent.

One end of the wire is placed in the earth
and the other is elevated in the air. The
height to which it is carried determines the
distance to which the messages may be sent.
The operator presses his key as in ordinary
telegraphing, making his alphabet in dots
and dashes. As the waves shoot out and
reach the distant station, the filings in the
tube cohere and the current passing through
them draws up the armature of the relay
magnet. This closes the circuit of the re-
cording instrument. It is broken constantly

by the tapper and instantly re-established by receiving waves.

The towers employed in 1920 for the transmission of wireless messages were very high. The manifest advantages of the system were apparent and long before 1930 wireless telegraphy came into general use. The new system proved the death-knell of telegraph poles, as well as ocean cables. Old telegraph stock faded in value like the morning mist. The supreme importance of communicating with vessels while at sea alone guaranteed the success of the wireless system.

Wireless telegraphy proved to be one of the crowning scientific achievements of the twentieth century, but the ambition of scientists in 1969 knew no bounds. In that year they were busy sending messages to Mars, utilizing starbeams for that purpose. For thirty long years they repeated the same messages or signals to Mars every night. In 1999 the canalers up in that bright Yankee planet had not yet responded but hope was still entertained that some sign of recognition might yet be secured from the Martians.

Chatting with the Boys in Mars.

Telescopes in 1999 had been vastly improved. The network of canals in Mars became far more distinct to the human eye. The moon, our nearest neighbor, looked as though only one mile away. Neptune, the giant of the heavens, grew on more intimate terms with our mother Earth, but on Mars was centered the greatest attention. Fervent were the hopes that Martians would acknowledge the ceaseless signals sent from earth.

The growth of the electrical machine industry in 1999 was enormous. The United States of the Americas led the world in their manufacture. The dawn of this vast industry was already manifest, even in 1899. The capital invested in electrical industries in that year was as follows :

	Invested Capital.
928 electric railways, aggregating 14,-850 miles,....................................	\$883,000,000
2,838 electric light central stations,....	335,486,518
25,000 private electric lighting plants,	87,500,000
Power transmission (750,000 motors in use)..	150,000,000
Electrical apparatus in mining,.........	125,000,000
Telegraph, telephone, &c.................	600,000,000
Total, ...	\$2,180,986,518

In 1999 nearly a third of the entire capital of the vast American Republic was invested in electrical interests of some form or other. The export trade of American machines became stupendous. The world demanded only the American make ; no substitutes would answer.

American pluck and brains proved the lever that Archimedes, the Greek mathematician, so long sighed for. American brains moved the world.

CHAPTER XIX.

CREMATION BECOMES A LAW.

No more grave robberies in the twentieth century. The old style of burial becomes a back number. Popular errors about Cremation removed. Undertakers at a discount. Costly funerals discouraged. Funeral etiquette in 1999. No person buried alive in the twentieth century. Sacred memories of the dead still jealously treasured. "Rented graves" and other burial abominations of the nineteenth century are forever banished.

THE great innovation of the twentieth century which long rankled within the human breast, but finally uprooted and conquered prejudice, was cremation. The old traditions and forms **No More** of Christian burial were **"Earth to Earth."** difficult to eradicate, but reason and a general sense of public safety finally broke down the barriers and traditions of ages. Cremation for many years shocked public sensibilities. The terrors of the hidden grave, nameless and horrible, were eliminated by the new and only safe process of disposing of the dead. In the contention which prevailed during the first half of the twentieth century, many were reluctant to accept cremation as the true mode of burial. By degrees, however, public opinion settled down and adjusting itself to the new conditions, accepted the quicker and safer methods of burial.

Cremation in 1999 became the only legalized form of burial. Every cemetery was provided with a crematory long before 1950.

Cremation Became a Law. Electricity was employed in reducing the body to ashes. Grave robberies that so often disgraced the nineteenth century, became impossible. A rich man was at least sure of a safe burial of his ashes after cremation, while the poor man's body, which formerly was thrust into a Potter's field, was safe at last from medical students and professional body-snatchers, who often robbed graves to secure a skeleton.

Rich and Poor on Equal Footing. Millionaires in the twentieth century enjoyed after death the same degree of safety vouchsafed to the poor man. Their dust was on equal footing.

The old graves were left undisturbed in 1999. Graves in that year, in the manner of their occupants, gradually passed into decay. In the centre of every cemetery was constructed a fine mausoleum, a pantheon in which the ashes of the dead were carefully deposited in vaults or family receptacles. Cremation having become in 1999 the only mode of burial authorized by law,

The State pays for All Burials. these mausoleums were built at the expense of the town. Each vault was owned by a family in perpetuity. Those who were too poor to purchase a vault had their ashes placed in a common burial plot in the ground.

These large mausoleums were built of white marble in a style of architecture appropriate to the solemnity of their purpose. The interior was well-lighted and ventilated and on the door of each vault was carved the family name. All mausoleums were built about on the same plan. From the centre of the structure arose a high dome of beautifully chiseled white marble, while light poured from the top into the circular floor of the structure. The vaults used as receptacles for the ashes were stationed about in a large circle, in several tiers, one above another. The ashes of the cremated body were deposited in a small metallic box, 9x18 inches, and four inches deep. On the cover was engraved the name, age, date of death and cremation of the deceased. Each family vault was capable of holding thirty metallic cases, or burials.

It was universally conceded that cremation was the only safe and proper mode of disposing of the dead. In 1999 people wondered how the ancient form of burial had so long been practiced by civilized nations. When in 1999 cremation became the only legal form of burial, they looked with feelings of horror upon the ancient form of interment. How people could lay away their loved ones in the cold ground to remain for years the

It Looked Heathenish to Them.

companion of the worm, could not be understood in the days of cremation. All arguments brought against burials in the ground were unanswerable. It was an offense against the laws of humanity, and the practice was maintained even as late as 1965, but public opinion became firm against it. The revolt against burials spread raidly, once inaugurated.

In 1965 a family that consented to the burial of their dead was regarded not only as a back number but with feelings of aversion.

Guarding the Bodies of Rich Men.

The question arose in the minds of many if they really could love the memory of their departed one and place the body where it was liable to be stolen or desecrated ; where it became the food of vermin. People in 1899 often had to even place strong guards over the tombs of rich relatives for fear that vandals might steal the body and retain it for ransom. Long after death bodies of men had been drawn from their tomb and hanged by a mob. When in 1899 Lord Kitchner, the Sidar of the British forces in Egypt, subdued and captured Khartoum,

Nineteenth Century Practices.

he permitted his men to violate the tomb of the Mahdi. The body of the Prophet was torn from its resting place and its head was decapitated. And this, note well, was done by British soldiers in 1899, to avenge the cruel death of Gen. Gordon.

In 1999 desecrations, robberies and violations of graves became impossible. The world was no longer shocked by such atrocities. Hyenas, both biped and quadruped, were thrown out of business. Cremation, the purest and swiftest mode of reducing the body to dust and ashes, was universally declared to be immeasurably better than the ancient mode of burial. The dead were not permitted to pollute the ground and to infuse germs of diseases, deadly microbes, into living springs of water. It matters

Everything For and Nothing Against It. little, in 1999, whether the cemetery were situate on top of a hill, in a valley or in the midst of a crowded city. The ashes they contained could pollute neither water, earth nor air. A mausoleum or cemetery in 1999 was often built in the most crowded or most fashionable section of a city. Cremation was acknowledged to be a clean, wholesome method of burying the dead. Boys in 1999 were not under the painful necessity while walking past a cemetery at night to whistle to keep up their courage.

In 1899 the popular idea about cremation was erroneous and was largely the cause of prejudice against this method of disposing of the dead. A vast number of people believed in that year that bodies which were cremated were literally roasted or reduced to ashes over a fierce fire. When people, however, began to learn the truth of the matter, that cremated bodies were placed in the retort of a crematory and were reduced to ashes by an exceedingly high temperature and not touched in any manner by fire, then prejudice let down the bars and cremations soon became common.

As a result of cremation and the law of 1999 which compelled its adoption as the only legal method of burial, undertakers **Undertakers Wear Long Faces.** were deprived of large revenues they often derived from the sale of caskets. Caskets were no longer in demand because, as a wag in 1985 observed : '' There is nobody to bury." A seven foot casket of the 1899 pattern, however gorgeous, would have been absurdly too large and meaningless to enshrine the ashes of a departed relative. Such contrivances were good enough in the backward age of the nineteenth century. Burials in 1899 were made under ground, while in 1999 they were all made above ground. In 1899, immediately after death in a family one of the first duties was to purchase a casket and arrange with an undertaker for the funeral. In their unhappy frame of mind, with hearts bowed in grief, undertakers often made terms their own way with mourners. Few mourners are in a state of mind to drive a bargain in such moments, and they too often yield to the blandishments of the suave casket-broker accepting any terms he may offer. Cremation did away

with this, and unscrupulous undertakers
had to come off their perch.

Hearses were not abolished in the days
of cremation. The style of the hearse
entirely changed. In the place of the pompous affair of 1899, bedecked in its towering
plumes, rich in silver appointments, massive
structures covered with
plate glass, driven by an
awe-inspiring individual
perched on a high seat,
the hearse of 1999 was a far less pretentious affair. It weighed no more than a
light, racing sulky. It had four wheels.
In the centre of the vehicle, which, of course,
was propelled by electricity, was constructed
a small platform about three feet square,
the sides of which were elaborately trimmed
in gold and silver ornaments. The platform
was covered by an open canopy supported
by four elaborate silver pillars. The metallic case containing the ashes of the deceased seldom exceeded 9x18 inches, 4
inches deep, and weighed about four pounds.
These metallic cases were of exquisite designs, usually in highly burnished silver or
gold. Those which contained the ashes of
the wealthier classes were often covered
with precious stones and brilliant gems,
presenting a most artistic and attractive
appearance. These burial cases looked like
jewel-boxes of an elaborate pattern. In
looking at them death was robbed of its
terrors. A beautiful jewel-case, 9x18 inches,

The Twentieth Century Hearse.

containing the ashes of some loved one did not strike one's imagination with the horror of a long burial casket with its inanimate tenant.

There was everything about cremation to appeal to loftier ideals. The light, portable character of the little cremation cases became more popular than the heavy casket. The heart-rending accidents that too often occurred under the old system of burials, became impossible in the brighter and better days of cremation. In 1899 it sometimes happened that in lowering a body into the grave the bottom of the casket gave way. The rest can better be imagined than described. It sometimes happened that **Sample Horrors of 1899.** while a funeral procession was on its way to the cemetery, the hearse team got frightened. In the thrilling runaway that followed the casket fell out of the hearse and breaking open the corpse rolled out on the ground. The horror-stricken relatives and friends would remember the sad scene through life, mentioning it only in whispers.

These horrors of the old-style, so-called Christian burials, were rendered impossible in the cremation regime. Not that alone, but cremation removed from earth the most horrible experience that can be endured by mortal man and that is premature burial. The practice of burying bodies is a relic of barbarism. Its horrors and possibilities are

without limit.   No civilized community
should tolerate it.   Custom and tradition
are the forces that maintain it.   It does not
possess a single point in its favor, while, on
the other hand, there are scores of sound
arguments against it.

No person who ever spent a minute in the
fierce temperature of a crematory ever

**Can't
Bury them
Alive.**

lived to tell the tale.
The ancient method of
burial is not so certain—
many cases have come to
light where people, supposed to be dead,
revived after interment.   Imagine the
horror of the situation.   Can any human
experience be more dreadful than this one ?
Many cases have come to light in the nineteenth century proving beyond a shadow of
doubt that unfortunate men and women had
been buried alive.   In graves opened many
weeks after burial the scratched face, torn
hair and imprint of terror upon the features
told only too plainly what had happened
and of the final anguish of the unfortunate
one.   Such horrors were not possible in the
cremation process.   If there is anything
the world appreciates it's a '' sure thing''—
and that salient feature of cremation did
not escape its attention.

On the day following the death of a person, after the remains had been viewed for
the last time by relatives and friends, the
body was taken by night to the crematory
where it was immediately reduced to ashes.

These were carefully deposited in a small
metallic burial case and returned to the

No Hurry for the Funeral. mortuary residence. The
date of the funeral was
agreed upon and notices
were sent out to the
public. Sometimes it was deemed desirable to hold the funeral one or two
months after death. In cremation funerals
everything passed off in the most leisurely
manner possible, accompanied with the
highest effects of art. A funeral could be
held a week, a month or a year after death.
There was ample time to make arrange-
ments, or to postpone a funeral on account
of the weather. On the day of interment
when the ashes were to be deposited in the
family vault in the mausoleum, at the appointed hour, friends and relatives gathered
at the mortuary residence. The small metallic casket containing the ashes of the deceased was usually placed in the centre of
the room, resting upon a light bamboo
stand, covered with black velvet. The
stand was usually surrounded with choice
flowers and floral designs. The tiniest caskets used in the old burial days were double
in size of the beautiful silver and gold cases
sometimes holding the ashes of a person
who might have weighed, during life, over
three hundred pounds. The absence of the
large casket used in old burial days and the
substitution in its place of a small jewel-
size case containing the ashes was an agree-

able innovation. Otherwise, all funeral services in 1999 were substantially the same as in 1899. Although the surroundings were far more pleasant, the grief of the stricken ones was none the less profound. When funerals in 1999 were held in a church, the exersises were about the same as in the days of the old burial system. Instead of six bearers, only one became necessary.

There was a marked contrast between the funeral processions of 1899 and those

Funeral Procession in 1999. of 1999. The great, cumbersome hearse had disappeared, and in the line of carriages that followed the small, light electric hearse, no horses were to be seen. All mourners' carriages were propelled by electricity. The automobile containing the minister, led the procession, then followed the hearse and carriages of the mourners. In 1999, when a funeral passed by, people on the streets at the time were always careful to remove their hats as a mark of respect to the ashes of the deceased. This was a concession to common decency almost wholly unknown in the days of burials. People living in 1899 should not be too severely criticised in their lack of respect for the dead in the matter of uncovering as a funeral procession passed by. The entire system was a relic of barbarism and people were hardly to blame for denying this mark of respect to such an objectionable mode of burial.

It was at first thought that cremation would destroy the sacred memories and observances of Memorial or Decoration Day. In a few years, however, it was discovered that these fears were unfounded.   People in 1999 were loyal to the sacred memory of departed ones, and on Memorial days the interior of the mausoleums and doors of the vaults were garlanded with flowers, presenting a most beautiful appearance.   The old graves of the nineteenth and preceding centuries were still cared for by loving hands.

Memorial Day in 1999.

These were decorated as in the good old days of 1899 and were not in anywise neglected.   Many families in the twentieth century took up the remains of their ancestors and caused them to be cremated in order that their ashes might rest in the same vault.   It was conceded that the ashes could never perish in a vault and another supreme advantage in favor of the cremation system arose from the fact that they required no care.

The abominations of the old fashioned burials were   apparently without limit. Under that barbaric system of the 19th century, it might truly be said that after death a man had not where to lay his head.

Ejected for Non-Payment of Rent.

One would think that after death a person had severed his connection with the living world. Such was not the case.   It often happened that men were taken out of their graves for non-payment of rent. That is, the lease or care of the ground not having been satisfied or paid, the ground or cemetery lot reverts to the Association, who dislodge the body of the tenant and offer the cemetery lot for sale to other parties. In the 19th century, especially in European cities, it was a common practice to lease a grave for five years, at the expiration of which period the grave was opened and the skeletons deposited in underground catacombs or left to the tender mercies of medical students. The barbarity of such practices, sanctioned by the civilization of the 19th century, need not be dwelt upon. Cremation removed the stigma of such unholiness from civilized nations. The ashes of the dead required no material space and were easily disposed of. No grave rentals or purchases were required in their case.

Last but not the least of the advantages of cremation was the death blow it gave to

Spoils the Ghost Business. the ghost industry. Superstition tottered when in 1999 graveyards had been abolished by law, as well as custom. The stately, white marble mausoleum which held the ashes of departed ones did not possess the gruesome appearance of the old fashioned cemeteries of 1899, with mounds and graves scattered in every direction, some of them in a condition of shameful neglect. There was something about a graveyard which was naturally repellent to the living. The ones who scoffed the loudest at ghosts, and were really very brave at noon time, were never favorably impressed with the idea of spending a few hours alone at night in a cemetery. When graveyards were abolished and bodies were promptly reduced to ashes after death, superstition began to weaken. Many people who would have been terrified at the suggestion of keeping a dead body in a house any unusual length of time, did not hesitate in many instances, to keep the ashes of several cremated members of the family for years, in their parlor. Cremation removed the sting of death, robbing it of its terrors. It was a blessing to the world and was thereafter ever sustained by enlightened ages.

CHAPTER XX.

NEWSPAPERS IN 1999.

They are still progressive and enterprising as ever and constitute one of the bulwarks of American liberties. The Pneumatic tube postal service and swift delivery of mails. Four daily deliveries of mail between Manhattan and San Francisco. A Submarine Railway Accident. A Marine Spider Crippled. Returns to Babyhood. Buying up Titles.

IT is the proud boast of America that as a nation it possesses a larger per centage of people who can read and write than any other nation on the habitable globe. Our excellent system of free schools and the ava-- lanche of newspapers that find their way into every home, at a mere nominal cost, have vouchsafed a general diffusion of knowledge throughout our great Republic. filling every branch of art, industry, and every profession with men and women of brains and intelligence.

The force and power of the newspapers in America in 1899, the perfect liberty of the press, were regarded

Safeguards of Liberty.

in that year as guarantees of public safety, mighty levers in forming public opinion. In 1999 the newspapers of the period had lost none of the prestige and influence they enjoyed in the old days of sail boats and steam engines. They were still handled in many instances with consummate skill and wielded a power that built, as well as shattered, governments.

In current topics and in the chronicles of events, there existed a marked difference between the newspapers of 1899 and those of 1999. New elements and conditions had come into play which were unknown in the period of the nineteenth century, and as a natural result the newspaper of the twentieth century contained some curious and interesting articles.

In 1899 the daily that got out a morning and evening edition was regarded as an up to date affair in every sense of the term, but in 1999 the newspaper world moved much faster. In a large daily office four complete editions were issued every day or once every six hours. The news poured into these daily offices with marvelous speed. Wireless telegraphy and ærial navigation annihilated space. On the other hand, newspaper and letter mails in 1999 were conveyed through much swifter channels.

The postal pneumatic tube system constructed by the American government was **Very Rapid Mail Deliveries.** a marvel of the twentieth century. There extended from Washington, (Mexico), a network of underground and overground pneumatic tubes reaching throughout the Americas, penetrating all the Northern, Central and Southern States, from the State of Alaska

to the State of Argentine. Mail deliveries
made through these pneumatic tubes were
exceedingly rapid. No electrical transit or
any method of ærial navigation could equal
the rapid delivery of the pneumatic tubes.
The mail pouches were forced through these
large tubes and delivered at all the principal cities in a very short space of time.
Mails from Manhattan to Washington, the
seat of the national government in the State
of Mexico, traversed the distance in less
than two hours. From Mexico to the State
of Argentine, as well as the Southwestern
American States of Peru and Chile, the mail
transit in 1999 required but a few hours
in delivery,—in 1899 it was a question of
weeks. Even ærial navigation in 1999
was found too slow to convey and deliver
the mails. The pneumatic tube system was
even swifter, and with such facilities at
hand it is not surprising that people in San
Francisco received four daily editions of the
Manhattan journals, although the distance
between Sandy Hook and the Golden Gate
is a matter of 3,600 miles.

The subjoined clippings from the *Electrical Times*, of Thursday, August 20, 1999,
The Editorial Blades of 1999. will give the reader a
general idea of the news-
papers, style and matter
of that period. It will
be observed that the noble race of beings
known as editors and newspaper reporters
was by no means extinct in 1999. The

subtle art of telling wonderful stories and the science of making American newspapers the foremost in the world, had been inherited by the children of 1999 from their lively ancestors of 1899.

In 1899 Yankee genius and enterprise was conspicuous in the newspaper line. It led the world. The latest and the best always found their way into American print.

FAILED TO BEAT THE RECORD.

How the Glimmerglass Failed to Cross the Atlantic in Two Days

LIVERPOOL, Eng., Aug. 20, 1999.—The new electrical ship Glimmerglass arrived here at 12:30, having made the ocean trip from Manhattan (formerly known as New York) in two days, eight hours and thirty-seven minutes, within twenty minutes of the swiftest time ever made by a wholly equipped electrical vessel. But for a storm of twenty hours out, the record would have undoubtedly been beaten. Owing to a break in the wind-counteracting engines, the storm in the locality of the ship could not be stilled and for over an hour the passage was very rough. The counteractors were finally put in motion and the Glimmerglass regained several lost hours, but the odds were too greatly against it. An attempt will be made to break the return record.

SUB-MARINE RAILWAY ACCIDENT!

Wreck of a Train in the English Channel Tubeway.

LONDON, England, Aug. 20, 1999.—Passengers on the Dover & Calais Sub-Marine Electric railway, train No. 44, arrived at Dover in a state of decided fright this morning. The sub-marine system runs directly under the English channel, the trains on the line of this company running through huge cylinders. At a point midway in the channel one of the inverted rails, owing probably to defective mechanism, had snapped in twain and the train, which was going at a high rate of speed, flew from the track.

Two carriages were overturned and the engineer was killed by being thrown violently from the cab. The passengers were forced to remain in the tube for an hour. Several in the overturned carriages were injured but none seriously.

MARINE SPIDER CRIPPLED.

Four of Her Legs Broken En Route to South Carolina.

Charleston, S. C., Aug. 20, 1999.—The marine spider, Nautilus, arrived here in bad shape from Brazil to-day, one of her fore legs having been broken. The Nautilus is one of the fleet of the South American Importing and Exporting Company, and was built at Charleston two years ago. The boats in this fleet were built on the principle of an insect, it being an established fact that a body can be carried over water much more rapidly than through it. The spiders were fashioned after the manner of a centipede, the feet being bell shaped and connected with a superstructural deck by ankle jointed pipes, through which, when necessary, a pressure of air could be forced down upon the enclosed surface of the water. The locomotion is like that of a pacing horse and great speed can be maintained. The marine spider had for its inventive source a treatise on its possibilities written by John Jacob Astor as early as 1894.

AMERICOMANIACS.

They Cause Much Distress in the Loyal British Heart.

London, Aug. 20, 1899.—Americomania is so far prevalent in this city that the deepest resentment is aroused in every loyal British heart. Since the wide-spread abolishment of titles and the very general purchase of historic castles and country seats by wealthy Americans, the foreign element has been a serious menace to English society, which has been for fifty years controled by the descendants of United States heiresses who married titles.

London swells are adopting the early western custom of wearing their trousers in their boots as a distinctive touch to their morning costumes and the sombrero is also being sold by leading hatters. Young debutantes are cultivating the unaffected manners of American girls, and many ambitious mothers are going so far as to send their daughters to Manhattan, Denver and San Francisco boarding schools.

MESSAGE FROM MARS.

ALARM LEST THE AMERICANS SHALL GAIN A FOOT-HOLD THERE.

GALVESTON, Texas Dec. 21.—The meteoric message which has been expected from the planet Mars for several days, and which the astonomers. located on Pikes Peak, Colorado, left Mars over two years ago, dropped in the bay off here to-day, striking the water with a sizzling sound. It was still quite hot when picked up and the metallic covering had to be broken up with an oceanic pile driver. The message was written on asbestos paper in non-fading ink, and a crude translation of it conveys the information that the high ruler of the combined continents of Mars died of gastronomic fright two years ago last November while watching an American Thanksgiving day celebration. He predicted before his death, that if the Americans ever got a foothold on this planet, they would ruin the incomparable digestion of every resident by the introduction of cranberry sauce. mince pie and plum pudding.

AIR SHIP MISSING.

THE STAR CHASER IS TEN DAYS OVERDUE AT TOKIO.

TOKIO, Japan, Aug. 20. 1999.—Transoceanic air ship Star Chaser has been overdue at this port for ten days.   It is feared that the ship has been caught in an upper ether current and carried many miles above her course.

As she has not dropped to earth anywhere, there is a strong probability that she has risen beyond the influence of the earth's gravitation and been drawn into the orbit of some neighboring planet.   Anxious friends of the passengers are besieging this office for tidings of the Star Chaser.

RETURNS TO BABYHOOD.

Tragic Transition of an Aged Spinster to a Drooling Infant.

Miss Imogene Elyria of No. 678,431,222 Four Hundred and Sixty-first street, took an overdose of Florida Age Regenerator this morning, and was instantly reduced to a squalling infant.   Miss Elyria was a maiden lady 45 years of age, and a few days ago she sent to Florida for a bottle of the regenerator to take for her complexion and to reduce her age a few years.

She did not, unfortunately, follow the proper directions, and one of her sisters, entering her bedroom this morning, found her reduced to the age of 1 year and crying for her breakfast.   She will be taken to the Oregon age-producing springs, where, it is hoped, the unfortunate lady may at least recover enough of her lost years to make her a blushing debutante.

A tragic feature of the affair is the fact that Miss Elyria was engaged to a wealthy widower, who is heart-broken at the terrible contretemps.

BUYING UP TITLES.

Extravagant Sums Paid to the Old English Nobility.

London, Aug. 20, 1999.—The English government to-day purchased the title of Lord Algernon Percy Augustus Dunraven for a mere song, the consideration being £10,000.   This removes one of the oldest titles existing in modern times and only about twenty remain in England. Since the law passed by Parliament providing for the purchase of old titles held by the descendants of the members of the peerage, as it existed under a monarchy, over £800,000,000 have been spent in buying up these remnants of a semi-civilized form of government. The highest price ever paid was that for the abolishment of the name borne by the duke of Argyle, £1,000,000.

Sir Tom Lipton, who will be henceforth known by the republican name of Thomas Timothy Tubbs, has been reduced to poverty by reckless expenditures entailed in his enthusiasm for air-yachting, and it is said that he has spent £40,000 in trying to increase the speed of his defective atmospheric racer, the Shamrock.

IT STILL INTOXICATES.

COLONEL WASHBURN OF KENTUCKY PREFERS DEATH TO NON-ALCOHOLIC LIQUOR.

FRANKFORT, Ky., Aug. 20, 1999.—"Foh one I shall not vote to destroy my Gawd given ancestral privilege to consume liquor, sah. They may call us uncivilized barbarians, if they will, sah ; they may call down upon our degenerate heads the unbottled wrath of the universe, but, as for me, sah, give me good old Kentucky bourbon, or give me death!"

With these words Colonel Henry Clay Washburn concluded his speech in the upper house of the legislature to-day on the bill to suppress the alcoholic liquor traffic in Kentucky. For years the annual legislative battle has centered on this issue.

Gradually state after state has abolished, what many considered an evil, and in most localities the effects of alcoholic drinks were destroyed by the chemical discovery which, when applied, made them non-intoxicating. But the Blue Grass state has remained firm as a rock, although in modern art and science it has no superior in advancement in the union. The bill under consideration to-day was defeated by an overwhelming vote.

The following advertisements, taken from *Sidney Record*, October 15, 1999, will interest our readers :

CLASSIFIED ADVERTISEMENTS.

MISCELLANEOUS.

It is not to be supposed that farming, the greatest of all American industries, had not made any progress during the twentieth century. Probably in no other field of labor was electricity employed to better advantage.

Farm Hands at a Discount.

FARMING IN 1999.

Farm hands in the nineteenth century were as unreliable in some cases as balky horses. The farm owner's distress and nightmare in 1899 was the farm laborer. But in 1999 the "farm hand" was practically done away with. Horses and farm laborers were no longer employed in the cultivation of the land. Electricity was on tap in every part of the farm. Even the milking and stable cleaning was done by mechanical means. In 1899 a farmer who hired all his work done and lived along comfortably on the proceeds **The Dignity of Labor.** of the property, was called by the absurd title of a "gentleman farmer." The farmer who rolls up his sleeves and toils is none the less a gentleman. A gentleman is not always the one who spends a life of leisure and lives on the toil of others. The hard working farmer in many cases proves to be the real gentleman ; he dignifies labor and commands the respect of his neighbors.

In 1999 all agriculturalists were "gentleman farmers." Their great slaves were the electrical machines. They never groaned, complained or knocked off work in the busy season to go on an excursion. The electrical farming implements could work all day without sitting under a shade tree, with a jug of cider and a corn-cob pipe. They labored patiently and faithfully and performed their tasks with great accuracy.

CHAPTER XXI.

TWENTIETH CENTURY INVENTIONS.

The Wonderful Automatic Valet,—a faithful servant
and silent friend. A Balloon-car Accident,—
twelve thrown out and killed. Excursion to the
Moon. Woman Worship in France. Ready Digested Dinners. Highly nutritious pellets for noon
lunch. Ice cream pills become popular; also
delicious fruit pellets.

IF some wide-awake American genius in
1999 had invented an electrical breathing
machine his invention would have been
well patronized. By the use of electrical
appliances, manual labor had been reduced
to a minimum. The electric automobiles,
ærodromes, ærocycles, electric bicycles and
hundreds of mechanical appliances used
as labor saving machinery, really invited
laziness. If a breathing apparatus had been
invented in 1999 its sales would have been
phenomenal.

In support of this statement we reproduce,
herewith, an article taken from the *Scientific American*, under date of May 28, 1999,
as follows :

THE UNIQUE MECHANICAL FIGURE THAT
DOES EVERYTHING BUT FEED
ITS OWNER.

Some years ago the need of a machine which
would dress persons on arising from bed, make their
toilet and prepare them for breakfast, or a stroll on
the street, was generally felt.

Several attempts were made to supply this want, but nothing was perfected until M. Pantalon announced the completion of his automatic valet. This machine was shaped very much like an ordinary man, except that it was built on an absolutely square plan. There were two upholstered legs, on which reposed a heavy, square chest, and above the chest was the head, also square and resembling a block.

MECHANISM OF THE VALET.

The machinery was directly in the center of the body-chest, controlling the movement of the legs and arms, the latter being round, four jointed and twenty-seven inches long. Instead of a face, the head bore a dial, on which the hour was depicted. The whole valet was wound up by a small crank in the back. If a man wished to be aroused, at, let it be said, 8 o'clock in the morning he adjusted the alarm button on a small dial on the face of the large clock at that hour.

Promptly at 8 o'clock the alarm in the head of the valet exploded, waking the sleeper. The first movement on the part of the valet after the alarm had sounded was to move quickly but noiselessly in the direction of the bath-room, where, by automatic stoppers, the water is set running, stopping instantly on the tub being filled.

AN AUTOMATIC BATH.

After turning on the water the valet moved back to the bed, threw the covers aside, and with one of its automatic arms gently lifted the man from his resting place, conveyed him to the bath room, laid his night robes aside and immersed him. The bath completed, the valet drew from its chest-cupboard two flesh-towels, with which it briskly rubbed the bather, and then again lifting him up carried him back into the bedroom, where it proceeded to dress him in clothes which had been laid in a certain place the night before.

From its automatic chest the valet took comb, brush and whisk broom, and in less time than would be ordinarily consumed in telling about it, the toilet was completed. A feature of the invention, as perfected by Pantalon, was the arrangement on the time dial by which the speed of the valet could be regulated, and a man could be dressed quickly or slowly, as he preferred. For busy men, M. Pantalon has invented valets that do the business in less than three minutes, including bath. The chief value of these valets is that, not being human, they cannot gossip, and every man may become a hero to his valet, provided the valet is automatic.

In 1999 the mania for saving time and obtaining rapid results simply knew no bounds. It is a wonder that the inventive genius of the Yankees was not applied to the perfection of some machine that would compel the universe to rotate more rapidly upon its axis. So great was the rush of human affairs that people found little time to eat. The feverish, mad rush of the age was intense. No better proof of this can be found than in the success of a peculiar enterprise, which in 1899 would have proved a flat failure. In the good old days of 1899 people at least took time to eat, but in 1999 a big company was capitalized to manufacture and sell Ready Digested Dinners. In order to save time, people often dined on a pill,—a small pellet which contained highly nutritious food. They had little inclination to stretch their legs under a table for an hour at a time while masticating an eight-course dinner.

Nutritious Pellets for Lunch.

The busy man in 1999 took a soup-pill or a concentrated meat-pill for his noon day lunch. He dispatched these while working at his desk. His fair typewriter enjoyed her office lunch in the same manner. Ice-cream pills were very popular,—all flavors,

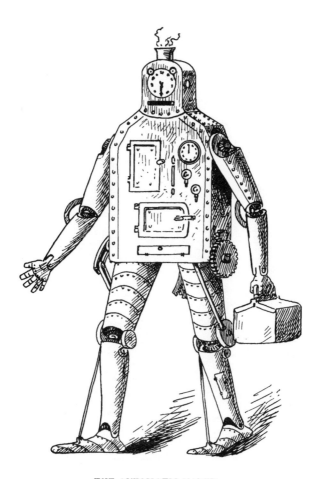

THE AUTOMATIC VALET.

also the fruit pellets.   These the blonde
and brunette typewriters of 1999 preferred
to the bouillon or consommé pellets.

CHAPTER XXII.

THE FINE ARTS IN 1999.

The art of Color-photography perfected in 1920!
The world's great artists witness the death-knel.
of art. The doom of cheap chromos. Nature
paints her own matchless pictures. The sculptor's art remains supreme in 1999. No machine
can ever chisel a Venus de Milo. No substitute
found for the human voice.

PAINTING, in 1999, had become a lost art, doomed, alas, never to revive. The glorious canvases of the old masters were still highly treasured. There still existed artists who threw their entire souls into beautiful paintings, superb creations of their artistic minds, true in every detail to nature Although painting as a high art still existed in 1999, yet, as a profession and a means of obtaining a livelihood, it died very much after the manner of wood engraving, when the half tone process was perfected and had come into general use.

In the year 1912, after many struggles and disappointments, Prof. Deweyton, of the Montpelier, (Vt.) University, perfected the process of color-photography. This coveted secret, at last, had been wrested from nature. For centuries her beauties had been admired but never had she consented to transfer her own original colors on photographic plates and canvas.

When the art of color photography was perfected, the world then had little use for

The Passing of the Artist. easels, palettes and painters. Nature became the Artist of the world and none dared to dispute her sway. At first it was with a feeling of sadness that the world parted with the art profession and its devotees, men and women who had imparted to canvas the world's historic scenes, the portraits of the world's great men, enchanting, noble women. The works of these great artists had delighted the children of men for many centuries. Raphael, Titian, Michael Angelo, Correggio, Guido, and other famous artists, had bequeathed their glorious treasures of art to a grateful world, and even color photographic pictures done by nature's own hand cannot rob these eminent artists of an iota of their fame. It was sad to think that after the discovery of color-photography great artists would lose their prestige, for none can rival nature in her own art.

This new process of Nature painting rendered to the world an invaluable service by

The Chromo Affliction Subsides. driving out of the market a flood of cheap pictures and chromos of the most inferior class ; pictures that had crept into many homes simply because they were cheap. These afflictions, too often paraded with flash moulding on the walls of our homes, were driven out by color-photography. In 1950 the old-style chromos were rare ; they quickly disappeared from the habitations of men.

Through the specially constructed cameras of Prof. Deweyton, life size pictures were secured, large landscape scenes, magnificent marine views, were reproduced w i t h t h e exact colors of nature. Superb sunset views, in a matchless wealth of color, a revelry of gold and crimson, were transferred to canvas by natural process in 1920. This process became the great art triumph of the twentieth century. No human hand had ever attempted with any hope of success to reproduce on canvas the bewitching and mystic effects of the gloaming. Nature with her master hand, dared to reproduce, on canvas, this most difficult of all artistic studies. Michael Angelo, the supreme chief of all living or dead artists, never attempted to reproduce on canvas Vesuvius in active eruption. No human power could do the faintest justice to such a scene and no master of the art ever cared to risk his reputation in the attempt. But in color-photographs Nature reproduced the exact colors of the seething flames as they belched forth from the quivering crater. In 1930 a magnificent picture of Vesuvius, Ætna or Stramboli in active eruption could be purchased for the pitiable sum of $50. So

Glorious Sunset Views.

perfectly natural were the volcanic flames that the effect was startling. The lava

Could Almost Smell the Sulphur.

running down the mountain side apparently threatened to set fire to the very walls of the room. A picture of this kind, a feeble representation painted by some eminent artist, would cost over $10,000.

The process of color-photography proved invaluable in reproducing human features and expression. Nothing could exceed the perfection the art attained in 1935. Photographic studios were crowded with work. No skill of man had ever transferred to canvas the maiden's blush, that emblem of purity, a shade Divine which mantles the brow of innocence only. The cameras of 1935 proved equal to that delicate task. The maid caught blushing in color photography blushed on, alas, forever. In detecting criminals, the new art proved invaluable. The Rogues' Gallery was soon filled with studies in life and deviltry, so natural that one's first impulse was to reach out for a pair of handcuffs.

Although painting, in 1999. and long before that date, had received a severe blow, the sculptor's art remained unchanged. The sculptor was still supreme in his domain. No machine had yet been found that could take a block of pure Parian marble and carve out a Venus de Milo. Nature had invaded the artist's studio and

robbed him of an honored profession, but
nature, great and mighty as she certainly
is, had not yet, in 1999, found â way to
fashion a block of cold marble into a thing
of beauty, an exact image of life.   Statuary
was still regarded in the twentieth century
as the acme of true art.   The sculptor had
not yet been dethroned ; it is doubtful if he
ever will be.   The new and most ingenious
machines of the twentieth century met their
Manila on statuary.   No machine can ever

Limits to Inventive Genius. be built that will reason
or think.   It requires
thought, judgment and
artistic taste to create a
statue.   As the artist beholds a perfect
model, he becomes thrilled with the love of
his art.   His heart and hands are guided
by fires of ambition and his work excites
admiration.   The human brain is often du-
plicated by machinery, but the equal of the
human heart, with its subtle emotions,
must ever remain a Sealed Book to cold,
unfeeling mechanism.

The same might be said of the human
voice.   In 1999, that peerless gift of God
to man, that wonderful channel through
which all emotions are expressed, had not
been uprooted by mechanism.   The Pattis,
Nordicas and Melbas of the twentieth century were still held in high esteem, commanding princely stipends.   The domain of
all mechanical music, however, had been
invaded to a large extent.   Pianos, organs,

orchestral and metallic instruments, which had attained a high degree of perfection in the nineteenth century, were generally discarded in the twentieth century. The tendency of the age favored mechanical music. The automatic musical instruments, which in 1889 had already attained a certain degree of perfection, were greatly improved. In the navy cornet bands were discarded and were substituted by large musical machines that played operas, marches, quicksteps, waltzes and patriotic airs with wonderful accuracy, with a volume of sound surpassing the best efforts of efficient brass bands. In the army, the brass band always held its own. The men who composed the band could march and fight, while no automatic substitute could be made to do this.

CHAPTER XXIII.

IMPROVEMENTS OF THE AGE.

The advantages of Electrical conveyances. No fire departments required and Insurance companies lose their grip. Tobacco chewing and spitting prohibited in public places. Cigarettes are condemned by law. Moderation in the use of wines. Great advancement in medical science. A purified stage. Religious toleration becomes more universal. Jews give Jerusalem the "marble heart."

THE changes in our social system that signalized the period of 1999 were marked and contrasted very favorably with the conditions extant in 1899.

Street noises that rendered city and often village life unendurable, in 1899 were en-

Uproar of Vehicles Abolished.

tirely abolished in 1999. The clattering of horses' hoofs became unknown in city life. Milk wagons, enormous furniture vans, the brewery wagon with its pyramid of beer kegs, rattling express carts, mail delivery wagons and thundering omnibuses no longer tortured the human ear in 1999. Automobiles had sent the clattering hoofs to Tophet and electricity, with pneumatic tires, was exclusively used in transportation.

It was a curious sight in 1999 to observe the life and animation of rapidly moving, yet noiseless, vehicles in city streets. Shout-

ing, whistling and all loud noises were
strictly prohibited on all public avenues.
The jingling of bells, the yells of street
Arabs, the thunder of wagon wheels over
pavements and the pandemonium that
reigned on all streets in 1899 became memories of a strange past.

The black pall of smoke that hovered
over manufacturing cities and darkened the

**Havanas
Cent
Apiece.**

lives of all men, had disappeared. Electricity
drove smoke back into
Hades and kept it there.
Manhattan, (formerly New York) the largest
and grandest city in the world in 1999, was
no longer troubled in this manner. The
only smoke that was ever seen in city or
country life curled up from Havana cigars,
of the best grades raised on American plan-
tations in Cuba and retailed in Manhattan
for one cent apiece. Pipes were occasionally used but had lost much of their former
popularity. Workmen and the poorest
classes could enjoy a fragrant Havana for
one cent and pipes were no longer used on
the mere pretence of economy.

In the 20th century the tobacco chewer's
life was not an enjoyable one. In many
States of the Americas, in 1999, notably
Brazil, East Canada and Argentina, it became a penal offense to chew tobacco in
public. In 1999 tobacco chewing was
everywhere regarded in the United States
of the Americas in the same light as opium

smoking. It was considered a filthy practice, one that must not be tolerated in
public. It was regarded as a danger to
public health for men to spit chewing tobacco on the street walks. Ladies in 1999
made up their minds that they had got
through stepping on tobacco quids on the
streets. Indeed, spitting had been prohibited in all public places. The habit was filthy
and dangerous, causing the spread of disease
germs. In 1980 it frequently happened
that the city police raided chewing tobacco
joints and hauled the offenders before court
for fine.

But, perhaps the worst form of smoking
was the diabolical cigarette. In 1899 it
Arrested was already sapping the
for Smoking youth of America, filling
Cigarettes. our hospitals with the
sick and our State asy-
lums with imbeciles. Great fears were
already entertained in 1899 as to the outcome, but public opinion did not realize the
danger to the national safety until 1912.
In 1921 Congress passed a law making the
sale, importation or manufacture of cigarettes a felony. Every inducement was
extended by National and State Legisla-
tures to encourage the growth of the purest
Havana and Manila tobaccos. The object
was to place a good, harmless cigar within
the reach of everyone and to discourage the
chewing and cigarette practices.

In 1999 moderation in the use of wines

and beverages became almost universal. Even in the State of Mexico and other tropical States of the Americas, drunkenness became almost unknown. In fact, it was regarded as a deep disgrace and a penal offense to be caught drunk in public. A drunken man was regarded in 1999 as a moral leper and was isolated from his fellow creatures for a period of one year and forever after was debarred from holding any public office. The law was sternly administered in every case which carried conviction.

The vicious laws of 1899 which allowed the government to collect an enormous revenue on spirituous liquors and permitted manufacturers to poison their victims with noxious liquids were greatly ameliorated. The National government took up the work of purification in the matter of manufacturing all liquors. A much purer and safer article, much less liable to injure one's health and to intoxicate, was placed on the market. It was recognized that the government could not regulate the appetites of people, but it determined to regulate the purity of the liquors they drank. This wise course produced a decided change for the better. Drunkenness was reduced to a minimum and homes were made happier. Although men still "drank" in 1999, none but an abject sot ever lost his mental balance and disturbed public peace.

Drunkenness Very Rare.

In 1999 vast strides of progress had been made in medicine and surgery, and disease had been eliminated to a very large extent from our social system.   Science attained a complete mastery over the hitherto unknown field of organisms. Man's mastery over these agents marked the greatest stride ever made in the conquest of mind over matter.   All classes of bacteria were held under perfect control. In 1999 contagious and infectious diseases occurred only in sporadic form.   The chief ills of life were those attendant upon old age.

Triumph of Mind Over Matter.

Specific organisms, namely those of construction and destruction, were created at will in that year, and were made to work with certain and perfect results.   In this manner disease was easily combated.

Fire departments in the city lost much of their old-time importance.   In 1999 only ten fire stations were required in the great metropolis of Manhattan.   In 1899 the population of New York was 3,500,000 and the number of its brave firemen ran up in the ten thousands.   In 1999 the population of Manhattan was nearly 25,000,000 souls, and its fire department required only three thousand firemen to operate it.   The reason for this is very simple.   In 1899 fire was used everywhere ; while in 1999 very few houses had any use for that element.   Electricity had completely abolished fire as a domestic agent or motive power. In 1999 people never ceased to marvel how their predecessors got along with so much fire, in one form or other, burning in their houses.

The sufferings of the poor in crowded city tenements during the fierce heats of summer, with a coal stove in their room, **Very Little Fire Used.** were recalled. The frightful heat took away all energy and appetite. Then the burning kerosene lamps were called to mind. Furnaces with roaring fires of coal, wood and oil, gas jets, matches, all helped to increase the percentage of danger. Fire departments were in great demand in the good old days of 1899, and insurance companies amassed fortunes by the side of which Monte Cristo was a mere Lazarus.

In those days fire not only constantly threatened the destruction of property, but many thousands of valuable lives were destroyed every year by that element. In 1899 women still clung to their long, dangerous and unhealthy skirts, long dresses that impeded their movements and exposed them to constant danger from fire. Fearful tales on land and sea were told of horrible sacrifices by fire. In 1999 all this was banished, never to return. Fires were extinguished everywhere. A safer and better element had taken its place. The Pharsees of India were, perhaps, the only people in 1999 who still " worshipped " fire.

Theatres in 1999 were extensively patronized, but so rigid were the laws against
immoral displays that none ventured to
violate. The cause of morality generally
had made strides of progress in the 20th
century. The world grew brighter and better and became more humane. Vice and
immorality were suppressed, not so much
by operation and fear of the law but by
Christianizing methods. As the world grew
older it became more manifest that crime
and immorality must make way for purity
and honesty. Theatrical performances in
1999 were more chaste, more attractive and
entertaining. The exhibitions of nudity, so

**No
Seeley Dinners
in 1999.**

common in 1899, became
unknown to the stage in
1999. Electricity was
very successfully em-
ployed in all scenic stage effects. Some
spectacular performances were beautiful
visions of fairyland. Public entertainments
carefully suppressed all that appealed to the
baser passions. In 1899 our churches and
theatres were still apart, but in 1999 so
marked was the purity of the stage and so
lofty its ideals, that church members were
not afraid to acknowledge that they attended
the theatres.

Churches, on the other hand, became
more Christianized in 1999. The envy,
wrath and jealousy which existed between
the denominations and religions lost much
of their acrimony in the 20th century. The

hatred and contempt that the Mohammedan

An Era of Fraternal Love.

entertained for the Christian, had greatly softened. The Roman Catholic, the Greek and Protestant Churches, followers of the same Saviour, regarded each other with more fraternal feelings and became more tolerant. As education became more generally diffused, humanity broadened the heart. Children in 1999 could not comprehend the infamy of a nation that could perpetrate the horrors of the Inquisition under a pretext of serving the cause of a gentle Christ. Their minds could not understand how in the 17th century both Protestants and Catholics burned, pillaged and destroyed one another's property ; burned men, women and children at the stake and committed nameless horrors, all under a sacriligious pretext of serving a Divine Master. These persecutions and the unfriendly feelings between opposing religions almost disappeared toward the close of the 20th century. The acrimony of the past was buried to a very large extent.

In 1899 the leading religions of the world, in point of numbers, were Buddhism, and the followers of Confucius, who in that year numbered 485,000,000 followers. Next in force of numbers at the close of the nineteenth century ranked the Christians, who numbered 454,729,151. The Mohammedans numbered in 1899 about 170,000,-

000, Brahmanists 139,000,000, and Pagans
or Heathens 220,000,000.

Christians were by far the most enlightened, most powerful and progressive re-

**Christianity
the Light
of the World.**

ligious element at the
close of the nineteenth
century and were firm
believers in the cause of
education.   Through their influence in the
twentieth century education became widely
diffused.   Turkey felt the force of the
movement, and the dense ignorance of its
population became more enlightened and
less cruel.   In 1999 the Christians of Armenia were no longer held in bondage.   The
horrible massacres of 1894 which so deeply
stirred the hearts of all nations were memories of the past.   The Sublime Porte had
ordered that education be made compulsory
between the ages of ten and fifteen years.
Through English influence the cause of education was also generally diffused throughout Africa.   Where education gained a
foothold superstition was uprooted.

Christianity made rapid advance in the
world in 1999, and Christians outnumbered
all other religious beliefs.   The sublime
gospel of the Cross dominated the human
family in that year, inspiring more love and
gentleness among men.   The vital force of
Christianity, perhaps little understood in
the nineteenth century, became a mighty
lever for good in the following century.
At the close of the twentieth century in-

dications pointed to a general christianizing of all peoples of the globe. The three leading powers of the world, the United States of the Americas, Great Britain and Russia, and in fact the whole of Europe, except Spain, which country was obliterated in 1930, as already described, exerted a mighty moral force upon the other nations. Even Japan was rapidly coming under the banner of the Cross.

In 1940 the ancient city of Jerusalem was delivered over into the keeping of a Christian power. All the territory about that ancient city, including the seaport of Jaffa, Bethlehem, the Mt. of Olives, and other localities made sacred by the Mantle of our glorious Saviour while on earth, were transferred by the Ottoman government into the safe keeping of the German people.

The Jews never returned to Jerusalem to rule again in that city. Centuries of persecution had driven them into every corner of the globe and under the protection of every flag. They had no use for Jerusalem in the twentieth century and nothing was farther from their minds than the re-establishment of the Jewish hierarchy. Their business had long been established all over the world and under no consideration could they be induced to return to the land of their forefathers, merely on a point of sentiment. Should the Messiah ever again return to earth, they argued, it mattered little whether they were huddled together in Jerusalem or scattered over the globe.

CHAPTER XXIV.

ARBITRATION.

It was not a complete but only a partial success. Certain international questions cannot be adjusted by arbitration. The losses of the American Civil War. Europe's terrible war record during the nineteenth century. The Great American Republic in 1999 has no use for arbitration.

IN the twentieth century many bloody wars were averted by the peaceful offices of arbitration. The Great Dream of Universal peace, however, had not been fully realized in 1999. In the political life of all nations controversies arise that cannot be left for adjudication to arbitration. Were it not so all disputations might be entrusted to the decision of the arbiter and the world would gain immensely by the abolition of the savage methods of war. A majority of the disputes between nations can be settled by arbitration, but not all. No tribunal of arbitration could have decided the issue in 1898 between America and Spain. It was a question of tyranny. Spain was determined

Questions That Cannot Be Arbitrated. to maintain a hell at our very doors in Cuba. That nation could not conquer Cuba and had proved, after over four hundred years, her utter inability to govern that island. In the face of wanton persecution, tyranny and merciless outrage perpetrated by Spain, would America have been justified in leaving its contention to arbitration? Certainly not.

When, in 1870, Count Beneditti, openly insulted the King of Prussia at Ems and aroused the indignation of all German subjects, what could Prussia do, leave the matter to arbitration? Impossible. After Napoleon escaped from the island of Elba and returned to France in 1815, ought the other nations of Europe which he had overrun with fire and sword, to have consented to arbitration as a means of quieting Europe? Certainly not. When in 1860 the Southern States of America seceded from the Union, declared their right of self government and privilege of perpetuating slavery, what tribunal of arbitration could have decided the issue between the North and South? None.

Human passions and ambitions did not change in the twentieth century. International **It Commanded Universal Respect.** al quarrels arose in the nineteenth century which could not be submitted to arbitration and war became the final resort. At the same time the world's call for arbitration, and the efforts made to enthrone Peace instead of War, never ceased to occupy the minds of twentieth century statesmen. The history of the world for centuries had been written in blood. The enormous standing armies of Europe were fast sapping the vitality and energy of those nations. Something had to be done to avert catastrophe and financial ruin and the Czar's call for a Peace Congress at the Hague, justly commanded the respect of the world.

War is a dreadful stain upon humanity. It is cruel, barbarous. The twentieth century was not equal to the task of entirely substituting peace for war, but made great progress in that direction.

In the nineteenth century the North spent $4,800,000,000 during the American Civil War, and the South spent $2,300,000,000. The number of casualties in the volunteer and regular armies of the United States during this war were as follows : Killed in battle, 67,056 ; died of wounds, 43,012 ; died of disease, 199,720 ; died from other causes, 40,154 ; total number of deaths, 349,944. The number of soldiers in the Confederate service, who died of wounds or disease, was about 133,800.

Cost of the American Civil War.

The world's plea for arbitration in the nineteenth ·and twentieth centuries was indeed a forceful one and the Peace Conference at the Hague in 1899 deserved absolute success.   It has been estimated that 40,000,-000 human beings perish in war every century.   Since the Trojan war (about 3,000 years ago), it is estimated that 1,000,200,-000 men have perished (up to the close of the nineteenth century) in battle.   The population of the world in 1899 was placed at

1,500,000,000. If all who had been killed in battle since the Trojan war could be ranged on a field and the entire population of the world also enumerated, the numbers of the killed would nearly equal those of the living.

In the 19th century in no direction was so much human energy wasted as in preparation for war or in the process of actual warfare. It was stupendous folly and a crime, a blot upon civilization. With such terrible figures before them the advocates of universal peace might well take heart at the sight of a Peace Conference, gathered in 1899 to adopt measures to reduce European armaments. During the last half of the 19th century the following great wars were waged :

War.	Cost.	Losses.
Italian (1859)	$300,000,000	45,000
Austro-Prussian (1866)	330,000,000	45,000
Crimean,	1,700,000,000	150,000
Russio-Turkish,	1,000,000,000	225,000
Franco-Prussian,	2,500,000,000	210,000
Zulu and Afghan,	300,000,000	40,000
American civil war,	7,100,000,000	800,000
Totals,	$13,230,000,000	1,515,000

These figures are frightful but they represent only a fraction of the losses of life and treasure through war, during the last half of the 19th century. The above figures do not include scores of other wars that occurred during that period. The Chino-Japanese war did not reduce the population of the Celestials to any apprecia-

ble extent but in loss of treasure it proved
a costly struggle.   The war between Spain

**A Story
only
Half Told.**

and America, commenc-
ing April 21st, and end-
ing October 26, 1898,
must also be reckoned in
this list.   The ceaseless tribal wars of Asia
and Africa, also the French colonial wars
in Madagascar, Tonquin, Siam, and the
endless struggles between savage races of
Borneo, Sumatra, the Zulus and head-
hunters of the Philippine islands must all be
included in the list of mortality from warfare
during the last half of the 19th century.

The plea for arbitration and the cessation
of war was a noble effort and a just tribute
to the civilization of the closing days of the
nineteenth century.   America lent her voice
in the cause of Peace at the Hague Conference.   In the interests of humanity this was
the proper course to follow.   America at
this conference represented 75,000,000 of
the most intelligent, brave and industrious
people on earth, whose army was a mere
corporal's guard.

In the twentieth century, however, the
great United States of the Americas, with

**America
a law
Unto Herself.**

its magnificent sweep of
territory extending from
Alaska to Patagonia, and
its national capital built
on the site of the city of Mexico, had little
use for arbitration.   In 1999 the vast American Republic had beome a world in itself.

It had long passed the period when it had become necessary to consult other nations on international questions and abide by their wishes. America in 1999 was a law unto herself, and had very little use for arbitration in the disposition of her international affairs.

Arbitration answers very well providing that the arbiters are just and impartial and prove themselves able to arrive at a decision in perfect justice and equity. But America in the twentieth century, on account of her enormous expansion and world-wide commerce, had excited the jealousy as well as cupidity of every other civilized nation, with the one exception of Great Britain. In any court of international arbitration in which America might appear either as a plaintiff or as a defendant, the chances were largely in favor of a decision being rendered against her.

America was denied justice in these international courts of arbitration. Left to the decision of European arbiters her case was invariably lost. Even in 1898 Europe's jealousy was ill-concealed. Germany and France would have been glad indeed to have assisted Spain in taming the Yankee and the rest of Europe, England excepted, would have applauded their interference. Because of England's firm stand Germany and France decided that prudence was the better part

Europe Becomes Jealous of America

of valor, and those two nations declined to have their navies blown out of salt water by the combined navies of England and America

If, as above evidenced, Europe regarded America in 1898 with feelings of envy and malice, imagine then the European condition of mind towards the great American Republic in 1999 when it contained a population of over 500,000,000 citizens, inclusive of a territory that represented nearly one-fourth of the habitable globe.

European nations in the twentieth century (always excepting Great Britain) would have been very glad, at any time, to attack and humble America, but so great was the power of our noble Republic in that era that even the combined assaults of the world could not have accomplished this feat.

As a natural consequence of this unfriendly feeling on the part of Europe, which grew in strength as time rolled on, America in the twentieth century withdrew from the International Court of Arbitration. America became big enough, strong and willing enough to take care of herself. In other words, throughout the twentieth century, Uncle Sam ran his own ranch and had things pretty much his own way.

CHAPTER XXV.

IMPROVED SOCIAL CONDITIONS.

Kissing prohibited in the twentieth century. The curbing of the tongue. The National punishment for wife beaters. The passing of the tramp. New methods of salutation. Vegetarians remain true to principle. Horse flesh as an article of food. Schools for training housekeepers. American hotels in 1999 still lead the world.

KISSING as a fine art was on the wane in the twentieth century. In the nineteenth century the Japanese had long banished that custom as one dangerous to health and as a medium for communicating infectious diseases. In that remarkable and highly progressive country no kisses, or salutation with the lips, are exchanged between husband and wife, parent and son, brother and sister.

The custom, without doubt, is an unwholesome one, yet one in vogue for so many centuries, even in the days of the Romans, that it became a second nature. In the nineteenth century one might as well attempt to scale Mt. Renier with a ladder as to endeavor to convince the mother of a new born babe that kissing is a dangerous habit. The lover in his rapturous mode expresses in a kiss the acme of his devotion. It seems cruel to destroy idols before whom

Kissing Strictly Prohibited.

we have bowed down and offered incense during a whole lifetime. Custom, tradition and education are hard task-masters. They cling to us through life like limpets to a rock.

Kissing, however, never came under ban of the law in the twentieth century, but the practice was discontinued on purely hygienic grounds. The mode of salutation in 1999 that was regarded as being the most tender expression of love, consisted of a gentle patting of the cheek. The advanced reason of the age broke the barriers of custom in this case ; lips were seldom allowed to touch lips. A pressure of the hand became ample compensation for the most ardent lovers, while the matchless language of the eyes left no room for doubt in a lover's breast that his love was reciprocated.

In the twentieth century men began to acknowledge the absolute folly of the cursing habit. If any excuse could ever be offered in palliation of this vicious habit it might be made in the case of a man whose mind was disturbed by angry passions. In an outburst of passion a slight pretext might be offered for the vigorous use of unwritten Anglo-Saxon. But the twentieth century very properly turned its face against the practice of verbal profanation. This reprehensible habit was made punishable, in every instance, by a heavy fine and imprisonment.

The Cursing Habit.

In the nineteenth century laws against profanity already existed, but they were a dead-letter on all of our statute books. In those days men might quarrel in public or in private ; they might hurl epithets at one another by the hour or by the day, so long as neither one of the belligerents raised a hand against the other, society and law took no cognizance of the unhappy occurrence. Men might exchange the vilest expressions and fill the air with their suphurious maledictions ; they might insult the public ear with a riot of profanation, no breach of the peace occurred in the eye of the law until blows were given or exchanged.

In the twentieth century it was finally discovered that the tongue was often a more offensive disturber of the peace than a blow of the fist. It was then recognized that vile expressions, particularly those which attacked innocent members of a family, were more cruel and cutting than blows delivered by hand or weapon. Society and law in the twentieth century determined to uproot and severely punish the offending of a vile tongue.

Wife-beaters in 1999 were speedily brought to time. These degraded specimens of humanity finally received their just dues on conviction. The lash which the State of Delaware wields to such excellent advantage in many criminal cases was generally regarded as inadequate punishment for such brutes. It was felt that wife-beaters should be made conspicuous examples before the community.

Every town in the Americas, from Alaska to Patagonia, was provided with a large **Punishment of Wife Beaters.** derrick, erected upon a solid stone foundation on the edge of some body of water. On the day and hour appointed for the execution of the sentence, the culprit was taken from the town jail or lock-up by the sheriff of the county. A large concourse of citizens usually gathered in the locality of the derrick to witness the "water cure" Arriving there, the sheriff adjusted two belts around the prisoner, one under his arms and the **A First-class Water Cure.** other about his loins. The belts were connected by a broad strap over the back, in the center of which was firmly fastened a large hook. This hook was fastened to the chain or rope of the derrick. Upon a given signal the prisoner was hoisted to the top of the arm of the derrick, which was then swung over the sheet of water. The windlass of the derrick was let loose and the prisoner plunged, usually a distance of twenty feet, into the water. He was then hoisted up again, and the dose repeated three more times. When the punishment was over the prisoner was properly cared for by the sheriff and his possé. He was conveyed in some vehicle back to the jail, where his ducking suit was removed. Attendants were on hand, who rubbed him dry and helped him put on his own clothes. He was then given refreshment and a cup of strong coffee and admonished to go forth and do better.

In the by-gone days of the eighteenth century, highwaymen, Dick Turpins, Jack **Highwaymen and Pirates.** Shepherds and the robber element, held high carnival, flourishing in their plenitude and zenith. The old stage coach days greatly favored the success of their profession. The appearance of steam ruined their avocation. The same fate befell the pirates of the high seas, marine highwaymen who thrived and carried on their nefarious trade in the days of sailing ships. When steam came into general use it became impossible for them to ply their trade. A steam pirate ship could not very well carry on operations. Frequent coaling and repairs to machinery soon revealed their identity.

The highwayman and his confrère, the pirate, were children of the 18th century. The conditions of that period favored their existence. They who would pursue the highwayman must have the swifter horse, otherwise pursuit became futile. The sailing man-of-war that would overtake the pirate must have a swifter keel or lose the race. But when came the days of steam these marauders by land and sea were driven from their lairs.

These were products of the 18th century, but it was in the 19th century that the tramp, a degenerate son of the bold thieves above mentioned, first saw the light

The Great American Tramp.

of day. The tramp of the 19th century, (an exclusive exotic of that era,)was a compound mixture of loafer and robber. He led a life of leisure. The law of that period rather encouraged his existence than otherwise. After roaming over the country during the open summer weather, as the first flakes of snow fell, the tramp, with the utmost ease, contrived to secure a six months' sentence in some county jail. Once safely ensconsed under the sheriff's wing for the winter months, he congratulated himself as a most favored

A Tramp's Paradise in 1899.

mortal. He was sure, above all things, of not having any work to do. That supreme misfortune having been averted, the tramp was at peace with the world. Work and soap were his deadly enemies ; could the jail save him from these, come what might, his serenity of mind remained undisturbed. He had a warm bed, three regular warm meals daily, with the privilege of playing cards, smoking and reading as suited best his fancy. What better could any tramp ask for ? The county jail was to him a haven of rest,—a paradise.

This delightful condition of affairs, however, rapidly changed in the 20th century. Society grew tired of turning county jails into tramp colleges, from which, after a very pleasant winter's rest, the tramp graduated in the spring and was again let loose upon the community. Tramps were compelled to work or starve in our county jails long before 1910. They were given plenty of stone to crush under suitable sheds, and the product of their labor contributed to better roads. After a few years, the new law had its effect. The tramp rapidly disappeared and monuments of stone were raised in every county jail to the memory of an extinct species.

The twentieth century method of exchanging salutations in public places was in marked contrast with the custom that obtained in the nineteenth century. During the latter period on meeting friends or acquaintances in public places, it was a custom established from time immemorial, when ladies and gentlemen met, for the gentleman to uncover by raising his hat.

New Style of Salutation. This was a graceful as well as a distinct act of courtesy. The l a d y, however, in nine cases out of ten, acknowledged the salutation, by merely looking in the direction of the one who had just saluted her. The lady occasionally added a smile in cases that were warranted by ties of friendship. These courtesies were graceful but in the twentieth century the ladies were the first to acknowledge that their method of salutation was ambiguous and indefinite. It was not as pronounced·and distinctive as the salutation accorded them by the sterner sex. Suspicion crept into the public mind that there was room for improvement in the exchange of salutation on both sides.

About the period of 1925 a radical change was effected. Upon meeting in public places, it was no longer customary for the gentleman to uncover, or for the lady to cast a glance in acknowledgement of his salutation. The mode was simplified. Ladies and gentlemen saluted one another in precisely the same manner. Each one, upon approach, raised their right hand in military salute, touching the hat, and by a quick movement, letting the hand drop to the side. This new custom placed both sexes upon equal and exact terms.

Whenever, in the twentieth century, a gentleman addressed a lady, after the usual military salutation, it was his duty to uncover and hold his hat in his right hand, regardless of the weather. Failure to do this would result in non-recognition on the part of the lady. The respect due to the fair sex perceptibly increased in the twentieth century and so must it ever increase as the world's civilization advances.

Man may be classed as being a carniverous animal. Vegetarians hold a different theory. They banish from their tables the flesh of beasts or birds that have been killed, eschewing meats of all kinds. It is the privilege of the vegetarian to live up to the dietary standard which he has adopted. Two-thirds of the human family take issue with the vegetarian on this subject. The vast majority are in favor of meats of all kinds as an article of food. In the nineteenth, and, in fact, in all the preceding centuries, the delicacies of the table most highly esteemed were those in which rare viands of every variety were included.

A model nineteenth century table reveled in such dishes as turbot à la cardinal, mutton chops, pork cutlets, lamb, spring chicken, selle-de mouton, ham, tongue, roast partridge, roast duck with sage dressing, turkey and cranberry sauce, braized mutton, deviled crabs, meat fritters, sausage, cold boiled ham. These savory meat dishes invariably played leading rôles at the tables of rich and poor. Vegetables and desserts were regarded as adjuncts to the feast.

A Standard of Food.

Vegetarians regard such food as alien to the human system and unnecessary to its sustenance. Added to this the vegetarians entertain a sentimental view of the meat-food question. They claim that man has no right to kill beast, fish, bird or fowl, to secure food supplies, and that all flesh food should be eliminated from the human system. A vegetarian's table was garnished with delightful dishes, such as sliced oranges, buttered toast, baked quinces, quaking omelet, shredded wheat biscuits, dates with quaker oats, fried hominy, stewed prunes, macaroni and cheese, stewed fig with whipped cream, French-fried potatoes, oyster plant and rice muffins. These dishes are clean and wholesome, although decidedly tame from certain points of view.

Vegetarians in 1999 were more emphatic in their views than their brethren of 1899.

Vegetarians Refuse to Wear Shoes. They still enjoyed peanut sandwiches, fried egg-plant steak, health crackers, nut biscuits, spiced beans and other delicacies dear to the hearts of those who have foresworn eating the flesh of " suffering, sentient things." In 1999 vegetarians refused to wear leather shoes. It came hard at first but shoes had to be sacrificed to principle. They refused to eat meat because it necessitated the killing of beast or fowl. On this account also they refused to wear shoes of leather because the beef must be killed in order to procure the leather. For the same reason vegetarians in 1999 refused to wear silk of any kind because its manufacture cost the lives of the dear little worms. They also refused, for the same reason, to carry alligator skin pocket books. It was so wrong to kill the poor alligators. Vegetarians claim that flesh is from ten to

twenty times more expensive than fruits or
cereals, and that it is unphilosophical and
unbusinesslike to pay the larger sum for
inferior food. Neither justice nor benevo-
lence can sanction the revolting cruelties
that are daily perpetrated in order to pam-
per perverted and unnatural appetites.
Vegetarians in 1999 were horrified at the
practices of the nineteenth century, when
butchers would take innocent little lambs,
the most harmless and pitiful creatures, and
cut their throats in the slaughter house.
The seas of blood that flowed through
Chicago slaughter pens had no attractions
for vegetarians.

In 1999 the world was by no means converted to any single theory or idea on the
food question. A delicious cold ham sand-
wich or slice of turkey with truffles still delighted the palates of millions in that year.
The savory hot bird, washed down with a
cold bottle, still held captive many epicu-
reans in the closing days of the twentieth
century. The birds of the air and beasts
of the field still contributed to the world's
gastronomic pleasures. In 1999 the vegetarian remained faithful to his creed.
Plum pudding, peaches in wine, haricots
vert, and other delicacies held the place of
honor at their tables.

But in 1999 the world became more liberal in its views on the meat-food question.
In the nineteenth century no argument
could shake the prejudice existing against

the consumption of horseflesh. Anyone in 1899 who could champion the use of

The Prejudice against Horseflesh. horseflesh and advocate its sale in open market on the same counter as hogs and poultry, would be regarded in the light of a barbarian or a person of unwholesome practice.

Such is the utter blindness of custom and prejudice that in 1899 the daintiest maiden, who might faint at the sight of a mouse, would occasionally smell the stench of a pig-sty, yet, without the least compunction, would sit at table and enjoy a pork chop, pork stew, pork roast, in fact pork in any form. At the mere mention of a horse roast or horse stew, the same delicate young lady would manifest her disdain, and if such dishes were set before her, her indignation might turn into riot. This was in 1899.

In 1999 people acquired more ''horse sense.'' Education, in time, broke down

Cleaner Than Hogs or Chickens. the barriers of pure prejudice and senseless custom. In that year it became recognized and fully acknowledged that the cleanest member of the animal kingdom, the horse, was fit food for human beings who had the strength of stomach to eat the hog, one of the filthiest, filth-devouring animals known to man, an animal whose flesh was regarded with horror by many branches of the

human family, animals into which our
Savior did not hesitate to cast devils.   In
1999 it was the universal belief that people
who could stomach pork and take their
chances in contracting trichinæ, could well
afford to digest the clean, wholesome flesh
of horses.   No animal has any cleaner
habits, or more wholesome food than the
horse.   Such is custom, habit and prejudice.   If our ancestors had taught us from
the days of the Cæsars to eat horse flesh
and to shun pork and poultry, it is more
than probable that a man caught eating the
latter would have been driven from any
community as a disgrace to his kind.

Prejudice and custom are hard task masters.   In 1925 it became a custom to eat
Eating Raw Fish. raw fish.   The fish in
such cases were carefully
cleaned before serving.
The head, entrails and
other parts were removed and the raw flesh
was served with salt and pepper.   Even
this simple process required an education.
Many with capricious stomachs revolted at
the treatment.   They could not digest raw
fish that had been killed and nicely cleaned
before eating, but they would readily eat
any quantity of raw oysters from the shell,
also clams, and eat them while the bivalves
were still alive.

The "servant question" reached a very
satisfactory solution long before 1999.   As
early as 1907, State Normal schools to

teach the culinary art and to educate servants were instituted. In the nineteenth century the servant class in America was the hoodoo of the housekeeper and homemaker. Thousands of young women in 1899, without the slightest knowledge or qualifications as housekeepers, entered into matrimony. Unable to cook a loaf of bread or make a simple biscuit, hardly knowing the

Some Very "Lame" Cooks.

difference between hot and cold water, these zealous but inexperienced wives suddenly discovered themselves in charge of a household and all its responsibilities. In this unhappy condition they relied upon hired help to do the work. In many instances the servant knew as little about cooking as her newly wedded mistress. It was a case of "the blind leading the blind," and much unhappiness resulted.

Early in the 20th century public exigencies demanded a radical change. The servant question advanced to the front. The dignity of her position was raised in the social scale. The backward civilization of 1899 treated the servant as a drudge or menial. Long hours of service, from early morn till late at night, were imposed upon her, while her wages were slender. In the country her life was more endurable because she was often treated as a member of the family. In cities, however, her lot was an unhappy one. The servant plodded along

in her solitary work, often busy and at work
fifteen hours every day. Even in free-born,
liberty-loving America the servant in 1899
was made to regard herself as an inferior
being.

It was in this chaotic condition of affairs
that schools for the instruction of housekeepers were opened and assisted by large
annuities from the State. Before 1950 every
town in the several States throughout the
Americas boasted of its State Cooking

**State Schools
for
Cooking.**
School. These schools
became very popular in
the Central American
States such as Mexico,
San Salvador, Costa Rica, Guatemala, as
well as in the southern States of Brazil, Argentina, Bolivia, Ecuador and others of that
group of the American Union. As a result
of this wise policy the fame and laurels of
French cookery were transferred to our
American culinary artists. Not even the
famed cooks of China could equal the skill
of the instructed and trained American
cooks. No servant could get a situation as
cook in 1999 unless they could produce a
diploma from a State School of Cookery.
They demanded more pay and were allowed
to work only eight hours per day. As a
result of having skilled housekeepers, homes
were rendered better and happier.

In 1999 America still remained the land
of model hotels. In the 19th century the
fame of Americans for maintaining the best

conducted and most palatial hostelries was already world-wide. Our city palace-hotels had no rivals in the world worthy of the name. In the twentieth century their enviable fame in this line continued to increase. Chicago and Manhattan still maintained their ancient rivalry in the hotel business. Many of the palace hotels of 1999 had walls built with opaque, rock face glass in the most attractive styles of architecture. From a distance they resembled fairy palaces. Marble and brick were occasionally employed in construction but glass came into high favor as being imperishable as well as highly ornamental. The old saying that "those who live in glass houses should not throw stones," answered very well in the 19th century, when glass houses, such as conservatories, were exceedingly fragile structures. In the 20th century no structures could be more durable than these hotels with glass walls, built with blocks of great thickness and in every color of the prism. They were fire-proof for the simple reason that no one had any use for fire in any hotel or public building in 1999. Electricity was employed to the exclusion of all other agencies for heating and lighting, as well as for motive power.

CHAPTER XXVI.

THE NEGRO QUESTION SETTLED.

Negroes in 1999 are transferred to their new reservation and permanent home in the State of Venezuela. The animosities between whites and blacks still existed in 1925. The negro a very costly importation. Never ought to have left Africa. In 1960 government lands are bought for the black race and their home in Venezuela becomes a prosperous and a happy one. The satisfactory solution of a vexed problem.

IN 1999 the negro problem no longer troubled the North American States. The absorption of the Central and South American Republics into the great American Union, had at last vouchsafed the earnestly prayed for outlet for the troublesome Ethiopians. The man who was guilty of making the first importation of negroes into the American Republic can never hope to rest comfortably in the great hereafter. The negro during the last half of the nineteenth century proved a black cloud in social and political America. A stupendous war was waged in his behalf. Years after the close of the war he still remained a source of bitter hatred and constant bloodshed. South of Mason and Dixon's line the war of the races raged furiously for nearly sixty years after the close of the Civil War in 1865. The whites despised, while the blacks detested. In

Literally a "Burning Question."

1899 Negroism was in fact, as well as in metaphor, a burning question. In 1925 mention was still frequently made of the burning of the negro Sam Hose, near Palmetto, in Georgia. Whenever the slightest pretext offered itself, negroes were lynched or burned alive at the stake. On the other hand these cruelties upon their race were naturally resented by the blacks, who lost no opportunity to make reprisals.

The negro proved a very costly luxury, a profound study in black, during the last half of the nineteenth century. Mainly on his account a Titanic struggle was waged in the sixties, a continent was torn asunder, 800,000 men killed and a debt of $7,100,-000,000 saddled on America, and in the opening days of the twentieth century, the negro was still a thorn in the nation's side.

A Study in Black. The negro found his way into America only after the mild race of Indians discovered by Columbus had been exterminated under the lash and torch of the Spaniard. When the harmless and gentle race of beings who inhabited the isles of the Caribbean sea had vanished before Spanish tyranny, then all eyes turned to Africa as the base of supplies for menials, hewers of wood and drawers of water. The docile nature of the negro rendered him available for purposes of serfdom. He proved submissive and obedient, which are qualities of excellence in the relations existing between master and slave. The negro, without doubt, is gifted with a high order of intelligence and is capable of appreciating all the advantages of a superior education. It is doubtful, however, if the race will ever become prominent in the field of art and sciences. With his amiable and submissive tendencies the negro is menial in his qualifications. For long centuries past he has been "a servant of servants" in his native land and his po-

Not Very Fierce, Only Humble. sition still remains unchanged. Had he the fierce and indomitable love of freedom which characterizes the North American Indian, the chains of slavery never would have blotted the fair name of America. His introduction into this hemisphere has proved a colossal blunder, a misfortune alike to both races.

History will applaud the wisdom of American statesmanship that emancipated the slave. No matter what may be his shortcomings—or how inferior his position in the scale of civilization, slavery of the negro cannot for one moment be tolerated under the great American flag, the emblem of freedom for all peoples of this earth. The flag, however, cannot guarantee his social status. From this point of view, the fact cannot be denied that the presence of the negro in North America is undesirable. In communities where his vote preponderates there will always be friction with the whites. Whites will never submit to the dictation of the black element. The swarthy son of Ham was never permitted in the twentieth century to dominate. The high white forehead cannot be ruled by the low black one. Not in centuries could this be accomplished, in fact, never.

The unquenchable hatred existing in the South found expression in frequent lynchings of negros, burnings and other barbarities. These acts of violence were deplorable, and even in 1950 the burning of Sam Hose in 1899 at Newman, Georgia, was constantly referred to. In justice, however, to the South, it must be said, that these lynchings were perpetrated as measures of self-defense.

The races could not assimilate. Miscegenation was regarded in the twentieth century, as well as in the nineteenth, as an unpardonable crime.

In 1925 the racial war between whites and blacks continued unabated, and would

Peace in Sight.

have still been in force in 1999 if the only one possible relief had not come at last to the rescue. In the year last mentioned the bulk of the black population disappeared from the North American States. The accession of the Central and South American Republics into the great American Union afforded the only possible solution to the vexed problem.

In 1960, just one hundred years after the Sumpter episode, another important movement was inaugurated in behalf of the blacks. People commenced to realize that the negro was an utterly alien race ; that when they landed here America gained nothing, while Africa must have lost heavily through their transfer into the new world. The proposition to transfer the negro population to the Central and Southern American States was agitated in that year. The transfer of Washington as the seat of our national government from the District of Columbia to the City of Mexico had the effect of drawing a strong tide of American emigration into the State of Mexico, and into the Southern States of Brazil and Venezuela as well. In 1999 Americans spoke of Colombia and Bolivar merely as Southern States of the Union. The vast and fertile lands in those States did not escape the attention of settlers. The idea of transferring the entire negro population from the Northern States of Florida, Georgia, Kentucky, Alabama, Louisiana, Virginia and the Carolinas to the Southern States of Brazil and Veneuzela was regarded as being a good one. The proposed measure proved a very popular one, particularly among the Gulf States. They were ready to make any sacrifice to be rid of their black neighbors.

In 1975 a bill passed through Congress appropriating a sum of $58,000,000 for the purchase of three northern provinces in the State of Venezuela, namely, Zarmora,

No Snowstorms out That Way. Bermudez and Miranda, bounded on the north by the Atlantic Ocean and on the south by the Orinoco River. It was generally conceded that the negro would feel more at home in a tropical climate. The three provinces named lie between the eighth and tenth degrees of north latitude, and there was no possible danger that these emigrants would ever get caught in a snowstorm on the plains of Venezuela. The northern States of the Union were determined to get rid of the entire race, if money ever could effect that purpose.

The negroes readily assented to the proposition and were heartily in favor of

Were Pleased with the Change. leaving a section of the American Republic which has been the scene of so much suffering to them, as well as their ancestors. They were elated over the prospect of emigrating to the State of Venezuela, where such a fine reservation had been purchased for them by enactment of Congress. They realized that in the State of Venezuela they would no longer be harrassed by their white neighbors and the old slave-owning element, and upon the vast pastoral plains of the Zarmora and Miranda provinces they would till their own soil, own the land and enjoy each other's exclusive society.   Even Boston, in 1975, applauded the movement as being a philanthropic one, calculated to increase the well being of the negro.   The brainy men of Boston argued that reservations had been frequently purchased for the use of Indians, and there was no good reason why one should not be purchased for the use of the American negro.

In this manner the vexed negro question was finally settled.   The States south of Mason and Dixon's line became more contented.   The negro reservation in Venezuela thrived well.   The broad pastoral plains, well watered by branches of the Orinoco, abounding in rich tropical grasses, were admirably adapted to the raising of cattle, sheep and goats.   Horses were raised in 1975 for food supplies alone.   The negro farmer invested in sugar cane, cotton, indigo and banana farms.   The tropical forests yielded much wealth, such as India rubber, tonka beans, copaiba and vanilla, while the mineral products of Venezuela proved rich and varied.

CHAPTER XXVII.

CONCLUSION.

IN setting forth at length the glorious achievements of the twentieth century, the Author has no desire to rob our now closing nineteenth century of one iota of its brilliantly earned laurels. The achievements of the nineteenth century will grow to the last syllable of recorded time. Their imprints upon the history of man is indelible and shall be linked in the chains of eternity.

In the field of scientific discovery the nineteenth century has no peer in all the preceding ages. It stands forth a giant whose achievements in the cause of science, liberty, education and humanity outweigh the combined products of all eras from the birth of Christ.

Newton's discovery of gravitation must ever memorize the seventeenth century in the annals of men, but the genius of the nineteenth century has produced its equal in the correlation and conservation of forces, the widest generalization that the human mind has yet attained.

The telescope of the eighteenth century is overbalanced by the spectroscope of the nineteenth, telling us of the composition, rate of speed of myriads of suns. The electric telegraph, the telephone, the phonograph, wireless telegraphy, and the Röentgen rays are all children of the nineteenth century.

The vast doctrine of organic evolution, the periodic law of chemistry, the molecular theory of gases, Kelvin's vortex theory of matter, are all priceless jewels in the crown of the nineteenth century. To these we must add in the nineteenth century phalanx the magnificent discovery of anæsthetics and antisceptic surgery, the wonderful mobilization of man through the medium of steam and electricity by land and sea.

Let us give to the nineteenth century the full measure of its magnificent conquests in the arts and sciences. But, to-day, we stand at the threshold of the twentieth century, in which, with its legacy of nineteenth century genius, still greater and more sweeping results will be attained. Vast fields of scientific research remain unexplored. Proud science must to-day bend her knee and confess ignorance in many problems of the most simple character. The absolute command of Mind over Matter calls for herculean strides of progress before its sway be undisputed.

The twentieth century, however, will preeminently outrank all preceding eras in the measure of liberty accorded to the peoples of the universe, and, in the foremost rank, as a pillar of fire by night and a cloud by day, the leadership of great, broad America will be followed by the nations of the world.

The Supreme Ruler of the universe, who holds this globe in the hollow of His Hand, has marked out the line this nation must follow and our duty must be done.

America is destined to become the Light of the World.

With her grand Constitution for guide and compass, her boundaries will extend until her banner of true freedom and liberty shall spread its folds and protect every nation in the Western Hemisphere, gathering them into one flock and one mighty Republic.

In the year of grace, 1999, the light of God's sun will reveal to the admiring gaze of the World, the noblest creation of Man, —a United America, the law giver unto the nations of the earth, a mighty power that shall dictate peace and banish war and make True Freedom ring throughout the world.